D1550758

THE ULTIMATE
Groom's Guide

THE MOST COMPREHENSIVE WEDDING
PLANNER FOR THE GROOM

BY
ELIZABETH & ALEX LLUCH

Professional Wedding Consultants and
Authors of Sixteen Best Selling Wedding Books

THE ULTIMATE GROOM'S GUIDE

Written by Elizabeth & Alex Lluch
Professional Wedding Consultants

Published by Wedding Solutions Publishing, Inc.
© Copyright 2005

The Ultimate Groom's Guide was Reviewed and Approved by:

Wilda Hyer,
California State Coordinator for the Association of Bridal
Consultants and owner of Events Plus,
Ceres, California

AND

Gayle Labenow,
New York Metro Coordinator for the Association of Bridal
Consultants and owner of You Are Cordially Invited,
Babylon, New York.

Information for *The Ultimate Honeymoon Planner*
was Researched and Compiled by:
Katherine Williams

Design By:
Sarah Jang, Wedding Solutions Publishing, Inc.

Printed in China
ISBN 1-887169-52-0

THE WEDDING OF

AND

TO BE MARRIED ON

AT

DEDICATED TO:

Brandon Lee
Movie actor and son of Bruce Lee, Martial Artist

The publisher of this book, Wedding Solutions, was planning the wedding of Mr. Lee when he was killed during the filming of the movie "The Crow," just two weeks before his wedding.

PHOTO CREDITS:

Cover photographs provided by:
Karen French
Karen French Photography
8351 Elmcrest Lane
Huntington Beach, CA 92646
(714) 734-6219
info@karenfrenchphotography.com
www.karenfrenchphotography.com

CONTENTS

INTRODUCTION 7

WEDDING PLANNING CHECKLIST 9

BUDGET ANALYSIS 21

FINANCIAL RESPONSIBILITIES 35

WEDDING PARTY RESPONSIBILITIES 37

ALL ABOUT DIAMONDS 45

NEWSPAPER ANNOUNCEMENTS 59

LEGAL MATTERS 61

GROOM'S FORMAL WEAR 65

GIFTS 69

CONTENTS

BACHELOR PARTY 71

REHEARSAL DINNER 75

THINGS TO BRING 77

WEDDING FORMATIONS 79

THE WEDDING DAY 85

TOASTS 87

DO'S AND DON'TS... 89

THINGS TO DO 97

THE ULTIMATE HONEYMOON PLANNER 103

INTRODUCTION

Congratulations on your engagement! You must be very excited for having found that special woman to share the rest of your life with. And you must be looking forward to what will be the happiest day of your life -- your wedding! Planning your wedding can be fun and exciting. But it can also be very stressful. That is why Wedding Solutions, a professional wedding planning company, created *The Ultimate Groom's Guide*.

Now, more than ever before, grooms are getting involved in the planning of their wedding. This can be very satisfying as it gives grooms the opportunity to voice their opinion about what kind of wedding they would like to have.

The Ultimate Groom's Guide starts with a detailed checklist of things to do. This list contains everything that a groom is either responsible for or should help his fiancée with. Discuss this list with your fiancée and decide who is going to do what. Remember, planning your wedding should be a joint effort.

CONTENTS

The book continues with descriptions of all aspects of the wedding a groom is traditionally responsible for. This book also includes a complete honeymoon planner to assist you and your bride in making your honeymoon as memorable and enjoyable as it can be.

We are confident that you will enjoy planning your wedding with the help of *The Ultimate Groom's Guide*.

If you have any comments about this book or suggestions to make, please write to us at: Wedding Solutions; 6347 Caminito Tenedor; San Diego, CA 92120. We listen to grooms like you -- that is why *The Ultimate Groom's Guide* has become an indispensable wedding guide for the groom!

Sincerely,

Alex A. Lluch

WEDDING PLANNING

CHECKLIST

The following Wedding Planning Checklist itemizes everything you need to do or consider when planning your wedding, and gives the best time frame in which to accomplish each activity.

This checklist assumes that you have nine months or more to plan your wedding. If your wedding is in less than nine months, just start at the beginning of the list and try to catch up as quickly as you can!

Use the boxes to the left of the items to check-off activities as you accomplish them. This will enable you to see your progress and help you determine what has been done and what still needs to be done.

WEDDING PLANNING CHECKLIST

NINE MONTHS & EARLIER

- ❏ Announce your engagement.
- ❏ Select a date for your wedding.
- ❏ Hire a professional wedding consultant.
- ❏ Determine the type of wedding you want:
  location, formality, time of day, number of guests, etc.
- ❏ Determine budget and how expenses will be shared.
- ❏ Develop a record-keeping system for payments made.
- ❏ Consolidate all guest lists: bride's, groom's, bride's
  family, groom's family, and organize as follows:
  1) those who must be invited
  2) those who should be invited
  3) those who would be nice to invite
- ❏ Decide if you want to include children among guests.
- ❏ Select and reserve ceremony site.
- ❏ Select and reserve your officiant.
- ❏ Select and reserve reception site.
- ❏ Send engagement notice with a photograph to your
  local newspaper.
- ❏ Buy a calendar and note all important activities:
  luncheons, parties, get-togethers, etc.
- ❏ If ceremony or reception is at home, arrange for home
  or garden improvements as needed.

NINE MONTHS & EARLIER cont.

- ❑ Order passport, visa or birth certificate, if needed for your honeymoon or marriage license.
- ❑ Select and book photographer.
- ❑ Select maid of honor, best man, bridesmaids and ushers (approx. one usher per 50 guests).

WEDDING PLANNING CHECKLIST

SIX TO NINE MONTHS BEFORE WEDDING

- ❏ Select flower girl and ring bearer.
- ❏ Give the *Wedding Party Responsibility Cards* to your wedding party. These are published by Wedding Solutions and are available at all major bookstores.
- ❏ Reserve wedding night bridal suite.
- ❏ Select and book caterer, if needed.
- ❏ Select and book ceremony musicians.
- ❏ Select and book reception musicians or DJ.
- ❏ Select and book videographer.
- ❏ Select and book florist.

FOUR TO SIX MONTHS BEFORE WEDDING

- ❏ Start shopping for your bride's wedding gift.
- ❏ Reserve rental items needed for ceremony & reception.
- ❏ Finalize guest list.
- ❏ Select and order wedding invitations, announcements and other stationery such as thank-you notes, wedding programs, and seating cards.
- ❏ Set date, time and location for your rehearsal dinner.
- ❏ Arrange accommodations for out-of-town guests.
- ❏ Start planning your honeymoon.

FOUR TO SIX MONTHS BEFORE WEDDING CONT.

- ❏ Select and book all miscellaneous services, i.e. gift attendant, valet parking, etc.
- ❏ Register for gifts.

TWO TO FOUR MONTHS BEFORE WEDDING

- ❏ Select and order wedding cake.
- ❏ Order party favors.
- ❏ Select and order room decorations.
- ❏ Purchase honeymoon attire & luggage.
- ❏ Select and book transportation for wedding day.
- ❏ Check blood test and marriage license requirements.
- ❏ Shop for wedding rings.
- ❏ Consider having your teeth cleaned.
- ❏ Consider writing a will and/or prenuptial agreement.
- ❏ Plan activities for your out-of-town guests both before and after the wedding.
- ❏ Purchase gifts for wedding attendants.

SIX TO EIGHT WEEKS BEFORE WEDDING

- ❑ Mail invitations. Include accommodation choices and a map to assist guests in finding the ceremony and reception sites.
- ❑ Finalize shopping for wedding day accessories such as toasting glasses, ring pillow, guest book, etc.
- ❑ Check with your local newspapers for wedding announcement requirements.
- ❑ Have your formal wedding portrait taken.
- ❑ Send wedding announcement & photograph to your local newspapers.
- ❑ Select and reserve wedding attire for groom, ushers, father of the bride and ring bearer.
- ❑ Select a guest book attendant. Decide where and when to have guests sign in.
- ❑ Mail invitations to rehearsal dinner.
- ❑ Get blood test and health certificate.
- ❑ Obtain marriage license.
- ❑ Finalize your menu, beverage and alcohol order with your caterer.

TWO TO SIX WEEKS BEFORE WEDDING

- ❏ Confirm ceremony details with your officiant.
- ❏ Finalize rehearsal dinner plans; arrange seating and write names on place cards, if desired.
- ❏ Make a detailed schedule for your wedding party.
- ❏ Make a detailed schedule for your service providers.
- ❏ Confirm details with all service providers, including attire. Give them a copy of your wedding schedule.
- ❏ Start packing for your honeymoon.
- ❏ Finalize addressing and stamping announcements.
- ❏ Decide if you want to form a receiving line. If so, determine when and where to form the line.
- ❏ Contact guests who haven't responded.
- ❏ Pick up rings and check for fit.
- ❏ Meet with photographer and confirm special photos you want taken.
- ❏ Meet with videographer and confirm special events or people you want videotaped.
- ❏ Meet with musicians and confirm music to be played during special events such as first dance.
- ❏ Remind your ushers of when and where to pick up their wedding attire.
- ❏ Determine ceremony seating for special guests. Give a list to the ushers.

TWO TO SIX WEEKS BEFORE WEDDING CONT.

❏ Plan reception room layout and seating with your reception site manager or caterer. Write names on place cards for arranged seating.

WEDDING PLANNING CHECKLIST

THE LAST WEEK

❏ Pick up wedding attire and make sure everything fits.

❏ Do final guest count and notify your caterer or reception site manager.

❏ Gather everything you will need for the rehearsal and wedding day as listed on pages 77-78.

❏ Arrange for someone to drive the getaway car.

❏ Review the schedule of events and last minute arrangements with your service providers.

❏ Confirm all honeymoon reservations and accommodations. Pick up tickets and travelers checks.

❏ Finish packing your suitcases for the honeymoon.

❏ Familiarize yourself with guests' names. It will help during the receiving line and reception.

❏ Have the Post Office hold your mail while you are away on your honeymoon.

THE REHEARSAL DAY

- ❑ Review list of things to bring to the rehearsal as listed on page 77.
- ❑ Put suitcases in getaway car.
- ❑ Give best man the officiant's fee and any other checks for service providers. Instruct him to deliver these checks the day of the wedding.
- ❑ Arrange for someone to bring accessories such as flower basket, ring pillow, guest book & pen, toasting glasses, cake cutting knife and napkins to the ceremony and reception.
- ❑ Arrange for someone to mail announcements the day after the wedding.
- ❑ Arrange for someone to return rental items such as tuxedos, slip and cake pillars after the wedding.
- ❑ Provide each member of your wedding party with a detailed schedule of events for the wedding day.
- ❑ Review ceremony seating with ushers.

THE WEDDING DAY

- ❏ Review list of things to bring to the ceremony as listed on pages 77-78.
- ❏ Give the bride's ring to the best man.
- ❏ Simply follow your detailed schedule of events.
- ❏ Relax and enjoy your wedding!

WEDDING PLANNING CHECKLIST

NOTES:

BUDGET ANALYSIS

This comprehensive Budget Analysis has been designed to provide you with all the expenses that can be incurred in any size wedding, including such hidden costs as taxes, gratuities and other "items" that can easily add up to thousands of dollars in a wedding. After you have completed this budget worksheet, you will have a clear idea of what your wedding will cost. You can then prioritize and allocate your expenses accordingly.

This budget is divided into fifteen categories:
Ceremony, Wedding Attire, Photography, Videography, Stationery, Reception, Music, Bakery, Flowers, Decorations, Transportation, Rental Items, Gifts, Parties and Miscellaneous.

At the beginning of each category, we have indicated the percentage of the wedding budget that is typically spent in that category, based on national averages.

BUDGET ANALYSIS

To determine the total cost of your wedding, estimate the amount of money you will spend on each item in the budget analysis and write that amount in the "Budget" column after each item. Items printed in italics are traditionally paid for by you or your family.

Add all the "Budget" amounts within each category and write that amount in the "Budget Subtotal" space at the end of each category. Then add all the "Subtotal" figures to come up with your final wedding budget. The "Actual" column is for you to input your actual expenses as you purchase items or hire your service providers. Writing down the actual expenses will help you stay within your budget.

If you find, after adding up all your "Budget Subtotals," that the total amount is more than you'd like to spend, simply decide which items are more important to you and adjust your expenses accordingly.

YOUR TOTAL WEDDING BUDGET $_____

CEREMONY

(Typical = 5% of Total Budget)	BUDGET	ACTUAL
Ceremony Site Fee	$_____	$_____
Officiant's Fee	$_____	$_____
Officiant's Gratuity	$_____	$_____
Guest Book, Pen, Penholder	$_____	$_____
Ring Bearer Pillow	$_____	$_____
Flower Girl Basket	$_____	$_____
Subtotal 1	$_____	$_____

Items in italics are traditionally paid for by the groom or his family.

BUDGET ANALYSIS

WEDDING ATTIRE

(Typical = 10% of Total Budget)	BUDGET	ACTUAL
Bridal Gown	$_____	$_____
Alterations	$_____	$_____
Headpiece & Veil	$_____	$_____
Gloves	$_____	$_____
Jewelry	$_____	$_____
Stockings	$_____	$_____
Garter	$_____	$_____
Shoes	$_____	$_____
Hairdresser	$_____	$_____
Makeup Artist	$_____	$_____
Manicure/Pedicure	$_____	$_____
Groom's Formal Wear	$_____	$_____
Subtotal 2	$_____	$_____

Items in italics are traditionally paid for by the groom or his family.

PHOTOGRAPHY

(Typical = 9% of Total Budget)	BUDGET	ACTUAL
Bride & Groom's Album	$_____	$_____
Parents' Album	$_____	$_____
Extra Prints	$_____	$_____
Proofs/Previews	$_____	$_____
Negatives	$_____	$_____
Engagement Photograph	$_____	$_____
Formal Bridal Portrait	$_____	$_____
Subtotal 3	$_____	$_____

VIDEOGRAPHY

(Typical = 5% of Total Budget)	BUDGET	ACTUAL
Main Video	$_____	$_____
Titles	$_____	$_____
Extra Hours	$_____	$_____
Photo Montage	$_____	$_____
Extra Copies	$_____	$_____
Subtotal 4	$_____	$_____

STATIONERY

(Typical = 4% of Total Budget)	BUDGET	ACTUAL
Invitations	$_____	$_____
Response Cards	$_____	$_____
Reception Cards	$_____	$_____
Ceremony Cards	$_____	$_____
Pew Cards	$_____	$_____
Seating/Place Cards	$_____	$_____
Rain Cards	$_____	$_____
Maps	$_____	$_____
Ceremony Programs	$_____	$_____
Announcements	$_____	$_____
Thank-You Notes	$_____	$_____
Stamps	$_____	$_____
Calligraphy	$_____	$_____
Napkins and Matchbooks	$_____	$_____
Subtotal 5	$_____	$_____

Items in italics are traditionally paid for by the groom or his family.

RECEPTION

(Typical = 35% of Total Budget)	BUDGET	ACTUAL
Reception Site Fee	$_____	$_____
Hors D' Oeuvres	$_____	$_____
Main Meal/Caterer	$_____	$_____
Liquor/ Beverages	$_____	$_____
Bartending/Bar Set-up Fee	$_____	$_____
Corkage Fee	$_____	$_____
Pour Coffee	$_____	$_____
Service Providers' Meals	$_____	$_____
Gratuity	$_____	$_____
Party Favors	$_____	$_____
Disposable Cameras	$_____	$_____
Rose Petals/Rice	$_____	$_____
Gift Attendant	$_____	$_____
Parking Fee/Valet Services	$_____	$_____
Subtotal 6	**$**_____	**$**_____

MUSIC

(Typical = 5% of Total Budget)	BUDGET	ACTUAL
Ceremony Music	$_____	$_____
Reception Music	$_____	$_____
Subtotal 7	$_____	$_____

BAKERY

(Typical = 2% of Total Budget)	BUDGET	ACTUAL
Wedding Cake	$_____	$_____
Groom's Cake	$_____	$_____
Cake Delivery & Set-up Fee	$_____	$_____
Cake-Cutting Fee	$_____	$_____
Cake Top	$_____	$_____
Cake Knife/Toast Glasses	$_____	$_____
Subtotal 8	$_____	$_____

Items in italics are traditionally paid for by the groom or his family.

FLOWERS

(Typical = 6% of Total Budget)	BUDGET	ACTUAL
BOUQUETS		
Bride's	$_____	$_____
Tossing	$_____	$_____
Maid of Honor's	$_____	$_____
Bridesmaids'	$_____	$_____
FLORAL HAIRPIECE		
Maid of Honor/ Bridesmaids'	$_____	$_____
Flower Girl's	$_____	$_____
CORSAGES		
Bride's Going Away	$_____	$_____
Other Family Members'	$_____	$_____
BOUTONNIERES		
Groom's	$_____	$_____
Ushers and Other Family's	$_____	$_____

FLOWERS (CONT.)	BUDGET	ACTUAL
CEREMONY SITE FLOWERS		
Main Altar	$_____	$_____
Alter Candelabra	$_____	$_____
Aisle Pews	$_____	$_____
RECEPTION SITE FLOWERS		
Reception Site	$_____	$_____
Head Table	$_____	$_____
Guest Tables	$_____	$_____
Buffet Table	$_____	$_____
Punch Table	$_____	$_____
Cake Table	$_____	$_____
Cake	$_____	$_____
Cake Knife	$_____	$_____
Toasting Glasses	$_____	$_____
Floral Delivery & Setup	$_____	$_____
Subtotal 9	**$_____**	**$_____**

Items in italics are traditionally paid for by the groom or his family.

DECORATIONS

(Typical = 3% of Total Budget)	BUDGET	ACTUAL
Table Centerpieces	$_____	$_____
Balloons	$_____	$_____
Subtotal 10	$_____	$_____

TRANSPORTATION

(Typical = 2% of Total Budget)	BUDGET	ACTUAL
Transportation	$_____	$_____
Subtotal 11	$_____	$_____

RENTAL ITEMS

(Typical = 3% of Total Budget)	BUDGET	ACTUAL
Bridal Slip	$_____	$_____
Ceremony Accessories	$_____	$_____
Tent/Canopy	$_____	$_____
Dance Floor	$_____	$_____

BUDGET ANALYSIS

RENTAL ITEMS (CONT.)	BUDGET	ACTUAL
Tables/Chairs	$_____	$_____
Linen/Tableware	$_____	$_____
Heaters	$_____	$_____
Lanterns	$_____	$_____
Other	$_____	$_____
Subtotal 12	$_____	$_____

GIFTS

(Typical = 3% of Total Budget)	BUDGET	ACTUAL
Bride's Gift	$_____	$_____
Groom's Gift	$_____	$_____
Bridesmaids' Gifts	$_____	$_____
Ushers' Gifts	$_____	$_____
Subtotal 13	$_____	$_____

Items in italics are traditionally paid for by the groom or his family.

PARTIES

(Typical = 4% of Total Budget)	BUDGET	ACTUAL
Bridesmaids' Luncheon	$_____	$_____
Rehearsal Dinner	$_____	$_____
Subtotal 14	**$_____**	**$_____**

MISCELLANEOUS

(Typical = 4% of Total Budget)	BUDGET	ACTUAL
Newspaper Announcement	$_____	$_____
Marriage License	$_____	$_____
Prenuptial Agreement	$_____	$_____
Bridal Gown Preservation	$_____	$_____
Bouquet Preservation	$_____	$_____
Wedding Consultant	$_____	$_____
Wedding Planning Software	$_____	$_____
Taxes	$_____	$_____
Subtotal 15	**$_____**	**$_____**

BUDGET ANALYSIS

TOTAL WEDDING BUDGET

(Add "Budget" & "Actual" Subtotals 1-15")

BUDGET $_____

ACTUAL $_____

NOTES: _____

_____

_____

_____

_____

_____

_____

_____

_____

_____

_____

_____

_____

FINANCIAL

RESPONSIBILITIES

The following are the typical financial responsibilities for you, your family and your attendants.

GROOM AND/OR GROOM'S FAMILY

- Own travel expenses and attire
- Rehearsal dinner
- Bride's gift
- Bride's wedding ring
- Gifts for groom's attendants
- Medical exam for groom including blood test
- Bride's bouquet and going away corsage
- Mothers' and grandmothers' corsages
- All boutonnieres
- Officiant's fee
- Marriage license
- Honeymoon expenses
- Groom's Cake
- Prenuptial agreement

FINANCIAL RESPONSIBILITIES

GROOM'S ATTENDANTS

- Own attire except flowers
- Travel expenses
- Bachelor party paid for by best man and ushers

WEDDING PARTY

RESPONSIBILITIES

Each member of your wedding party has his/her own individual duties and responsibilities. The following is a list of the most important duties for each member of your wedding party.

The best and most convenient method of conveying this information to members of your wedding party is by purchasing a set of the *Wedding Party Responsibility Cards* published by Wedding Solutions.

These cards are very attractive and contain all the information your wedding party needs to know to assure a smooth wedding; i.e., what to do, how to do it, when to do it, when to arrive, and much more. They also include Financial Responsibilities as well as the Processional, Recessional and Altar line-ups.

BEST MAN

- Responsible for organizing ushers' activities.
- Organizes bachelor party for groom.
- Drives groom to ceremony site and sees that he is properly dressed before the wedding.
- Arrives dressed at ceremony site 1 hour before the wedding for photographs.
- Brings marriage license to wedding.
- Pays the clergyman, musicians, photographer, and any other service providers the day of the wedding.
- Holds the bride's ring for the groom, if no ring bearer, until needed by officiant.
- Witnesses the signing of the marriage license.
- Drives newlyweds to reception if no hired driver.
- Offers first toast at reception, usually before dinner.
- Keeps groom on schedule.
- Dances with maid of honor during the bridal party dance.

BEST MAN (CONT.)

- May drive couple to airport or honeymoon suite.
- Oversees return of tuxedo rentals for groom and ushers, on time and in good condition.

WEDDING PARTY RESPONSIBILITIES

USHERS

- Help best man with bachelor party.
- Arrive dressed at ceremony site 1 hour before the wedding for photographs.
- Distribute wedding programs and maps to the reception as guests arrive.
- Seat guests at the ceremony as follows:
  - -- If female, offer the right arm.
  - -- If male, walk along his left side.
  - -- If couple, offer right arm to female; male follows a step or two behind.
  - -- Seat bride's guests in left pews.
  - -- Seat groom's guests in right pews.
  - -- Maintain equal number of guests in left and right pews, if possible.
  - -- Should a group of guests arrive at the same time, seat the eldest woman first.
  - -- Just prior to the processional, escort groom's mother to her seat; then escort bride's mother to her seat.
- Two ushers may roll carpet down the aisle after both mothers are seated.
- If pew ribbons are used, two ushers may loosen them one row at a time after the ceremony.

USHERS (CONT.)

- Direct guests to the reception site.
- Dance with bridesmaids and other important guests.

GROOM'S MOTHER

- Helps prepare guest list for groom and his family.
- Selects attire that complements mother of the bride's attire.
- Makes accommodations for groom's out-of-town guests.
- With groom's father, plans rehearsal dinner.
- Arrives dressed at ceremony site 1 hour before the wedding for photographs.
- May stand up to signal the start of the processional.
- Can witness the signing of the marriage license.

GROOM'S FATHER

- Helps prepare guest list for groom and his family.
- Selects attire that complements groom's attire.
- With groom's mother, plans rehearsal dinner.
- Offers toast to bride at rehearsal dinner.
- Arrives dressed at ceremony site 1 hour before the wedding for photographs.
- Can witness the signing of the marriage license.

WEDDING PARTY RESPONSIBILITIES

NOTES:

ALL ABOUT DIAMONDS

Throughout the world, diamonds are used to symbolize love and the unbreakable bond of marriage. Searching for a diamond, however, can be very stressful since there are many factors that can affect your decision, such as shape, size, beauty and cost. The following information will give you the knowledge you need to make that very special purchase.

DIAMOND SHAPES

There are various shapes of diamonds. The most popular is the round cut, known as "brilliant." Close to 75 percent of diamonds sold are round. This is mainly because they tend to sparkle more than the other shapes. Other shapes, such as marquise, oval, emerald, princess (or square), and the pear shape, are known as "fancy."

ALL ABOUT DIAMONDS

BEFORE YOU BUY

Before purchasing a diamond, you will need to know your fiancée's taste. If you are planning to surprise her, try to purchase your diamond from a reputable source that offers a money back guarantee or at least allows exchange.

DIAMOND LINGO

Boat: The boat is a piece of paper used to hold the diamond upright (in a V-shape) so one can look at the diamond. This paper is extremely white so it allows you to see the diamond's true color.

Brilliance: Brilliance is the amount of sparkle a diamond possesses.

Chips: Chips are external nicks in the girdle of the diamond.

Clouds: Clouds refer to a cloudy area inside the diamond.

Crown: The crown is the part of the diamond above the girdle.

Culet: The culet is the minute bottom facet of the stone.

Facets: Facets are the planes on a diamond which direct light through the stone.

Feathers: Feathers are used to describe a central crack with little cracks along its side.

Fire: Fire is the intensity of colors created by a diamond.

Girdle : The girdle is the rim or edge of the stone having the largest diameter.

Inclusions: Inclusions are the carbon spots inside a diamond which reflect light, making the spot look black.

Scratch: A scratch is a mark on the face of the diamond. Scratches can usually be polished out.

Pavilion: The pavilion is the part of the diamond below the girdle.

Table: The table is the broad top facet of the diamond.

DRAWING OF A DIAMOND

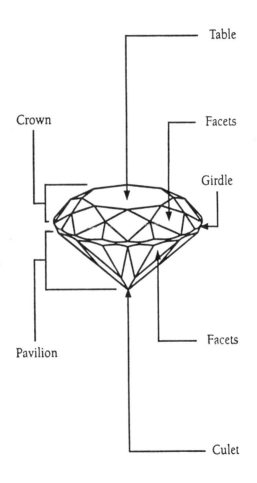

THE FOUR C's

The famous four C's are the main characteristics that determine the value of a diamond. They refer to color, cut, clarity and carat.

COLOR

A diamond's color scale ranges from D to Z.

D to F: ....Colorless

G to J: ....Near colorless

K to M: ....Faint yellow

N to R: ....Very light yellow

S to Z:..Light yellow

Z+: ....Fancy or colored

Keep in mind that the slight color of near colorless diamonds is usually visible only through a magnifying lens and from the underside of the diamond. Therefore, minor shades of color, even in diamonds in the I category, are hard to see in mounted stones.

CUT

Cut is the most important element of a diamond. It is what gives the diamond fire and sparkle. Most women would agree that a smaller diamond with a lot of fire and sparkle is better than a bigger diamond without any flair.

A diamond that is cut too shallow may appear larger than a properly cut diamond of the same size, but it may have less sparkle. On the other hand, a diamond that is cut too deep may appear smaller than a properly cut diamond of the same size, but it may look darker.

Prices can vary as much as 50 percent between a well-cut stone and a poorly-cut stone.

CLARITY

The clarity of the diamond is also very important as it

allows you to see the diamond's level of perfection. The more imperfections in a diamond, the less fire or sparkle it has. The less imperfections in a diamond, the more light that can pass through it.

Clarity is graded on a scale of Flawless (FL), Internally Flawless (IF), Very Very Slight Inclusion (VVS1 and VVS2), Very Slight Inclusion (VSl and VS2), and Slight Inclusion (SI1-SI3). Clarity is always graded under a jeweler's loupe (10x magnification) and always with an experienced eye.

FLAWS OR INCLUSIONS

All diamonds have one or more inclusions, whether visible or not, but no two diamonds have the same inclusion in the same area. Therefore, flaws or inclusions are often referred to as the "fingerprint" of the diamond.

Flawless (FL)
An FL diamond contains no imperfections. These diamonds are extremely rare and therefore very expensive.

Internally flawless (IF)
An IF diamond has no internal inclusions and very few minor external inclusions.

Very Very Slight Inclusions (VVS1)

A VVS1 diamond has very small inclusions, mainly externally. These inclusions are so small that they are hard to find even with a jeweler's loupe.

Very Very Slight Inclusions (VVS2)

A VVS2 diamond has a little larger inclusion than the VVS1 but it is still hard to see under a jeweler's loupe.

Very Slight Inclusions 1 (VS1)

A VS1 diamond has small inclusions, usually around the edge of the stone. It is not easy to see these inclusions under a jeweler's loupe.

Very Slight Inclusions 2 (VS2)

A VS2 diamond has small inclusions, usually around the heart of the stone. These inclusions may be a little difficult to see under a jeweler's loupe.

Slight Inclusions 1 (SI1)

An SI1 diamond has few inclusions, usually around the edge of the diamond. These inclusions are easy to locate under a jeweler's loupe.

Slight Inclusions 2 (SI2)

An SI2 diamond has inclusions, usually around the table of the diamond. These inclusions are very easy to locate under a jeweler's loupe.

Slight Inclusions 3 (SI3)

An SI3 diamond has inclusions, usually under the table of the diamond. These inclusions are very easy to locate under a jeweler's loupe.

Inclusions 1 (I1)

An I1 diamond has several inclusions inside the diamond that are very easy to locate under a jeweler's loupe and may even be seen with the naked eye.

Inclusions 2 (I2)

An I2 diamond has several inclusions, usually in the heart of the stone. These inclusions are easily seen by the naked eye.

Inclusions 3 (I3)

An I3 diamond has several inclusions that are very easily seen by the naked eye.

ALL ABOUT DIAMONDS

CARAT

Carat is the unit used to measure the weight of a diamond. It is equal to 200 milligrams or 142 carats to the ounce. The cost of a diamond increases exponentially as its size or weight increases. For example, a two-carat diamond costs much more than two one-carat diamonds. This is because bigger diamonds are harder to find.

The price point for a carat is about .85-carat. This means that a .80 carat diamond will cost much less than a .90 carat diamond, but a .90 carat diamond will cost almost the same as a 1 carat diamond. So if you have the choice, buy either a .80 carat diamond or, if you can afford it, a 1 carat diamond.

To save money, set a small side diamond on each side of the center diamond; this will make the center stone look much bigger. Or buy an oval diamond, which is the least expensive shape. Buy your diamond after Christmas or Valentine's Day to take advantage of sales. Summer is also a good time to buy a diamond since jewelers are usually slow during this time.

Keep in mind that color is not too crucial since it is difficult to discern color differences once the diamond is mounted. Beware of buying a diamond from a fly-by-night operation. Buy from a reputable jeweler who offers a money-back guarantee or at least gives you the option of trading-in your diamond for another one. And make your purchase subject to verification of GIA certification.

Do not rely on verification by a GIA-certified agent recommended by the jeweler who sold you the diamond. Try to find an independent agent or go directly to the GIA. The GIA is the only independent organization which will tell you the true, unbiased characteristics of your diamond without having an interest in selling you something.

BEFORE YOU BUY

Before you purchase a diamond, make sure you get a detailed appraisal of the diamond in writing. Also get in writing any other policy such as money-back or trade-in as well as whether the purchase is subject to verification of GIA certification.

When shopping for a diamond, use the following tables to compare diamonds from various sources.

DIAMOND COMPARISON CHART

Name of Source:

Color:

Cut:

Clarity:

Carat:

Cost:

Name of Source:

Color:

Cut:

Clarity:

Carat:

Cost:

Name of Source:

Color:

Cut:

Clarity:

Carat:

Cost:

DIAMOND COMPARISON CHART

Name of Source:

Color:

Cut:

Clarity:

Carat:

Cost:

Name of Source:

Color:

Cut:

Clarity:

Carat:

Cost:

Name of Source:

Color:

Cut:

Clarity:

Carat:

Cost:

DIAMOND COMPARISON CHART

Name of Source:

Color:

Cut:

Clarity:

Carat:

Cost:

Name of Source:

Color:

Cut:

Clarity:

Carat:

Cost:

Name of Source:

Color:

Cut:

Clarity:

Carat:

Cost:

NEWSPAPER

ANNOUNCEMENTS

There are two types of announcements you can send to your local newspaper: one to announce your engagement, and one to announce your wedding.

For your engagement announcement, send information to the newspapers, along with a photograph, right after your engagement or at least 4 to 6 weeks before the wedding. The photograph is usually the head and shoulders of the engaged couple.

The photograph should be wallet-sized or larger, black and white and glossy. Call your local newspapers to ask about their requirements. Most papers will not take orders over the phone, so you will need to mail the information or deliver it personally.

For your wedding announcement, send information to the newspapers, along with a photograph of either the bride alone or both of you together, at least three weeks before the wedding. The photograph should be wallet-sized or larger, black and white, and glossy. Your photograph should show the way you will look the day of your wedding. The announcement should appear the day following the ceremony.

If you and your fiancée grew up in different towns, consider sending announcements to the local papers of both towns. If either of you is having second thoughts about the wedding, cancel both announcements as soon as possible.

If you don't mind having your wedding announced a few weeks after the wedding, you can send a photo from your actual wedding day. This will save you the cost and hassle of dressing up to have your photo taken before the wedding.

LEGAL MATTERS

MARRIAGE LICENSE

Marriage license requirements are state-regulated and may be obtained from the County Clerk in most county courthouses.

Some states (California and Nevada, for example) offer two types of marriage licenses: a public license and a confidential one. The public license is the most common one and requires a health certificate. This license can only be obtained at the County Clerk's office.

The confidential license is usually less expensive and does not require a health certificate. If offered, it can usually be obtained from most Justices of the Peace. An oath must be taken in order to receive either license.

Requirements vary from state to state but generally include the following points:

LEGAL MATTERS

1. Applying for and paying the fee for the marriage license. There is usually a waiting period before the license is valid and a limited time before it expires.

2. Meeting residency requirements of the state and/or county where the ceremony will take place.

3. Meeting the legal age requirements for both bride and groom or having parental consent.

4. Presenting any required identification, birth or baptismal certificates, marriage eligibility or other documents.

5. Obtaining a medical examination and/or blood test for both the bride and groom to detect communicable diseases.

PRENUPTIAL AGREEMENT

A prenuptial agreement is a legal contract between the bride and groom itemizing the property each brings into the marriage and explaining how those properties will be divided in case of divorce or death. Although you can write your own agreement, it is advisable to have an attorney draw up or review the document. The two of you should be represented by different attorneys.

Consider a prenuptial agreement if one or both of you have a significant amount of capital or assets, or if there are children involved from a previous marriage. If you are going to live in a different state after your wedding, consider having an attorney from that state draw up or review your document.

Nobody likes to talk about divorce or death when planning a wedding, but it is very important to give these issues your utmost consideration. By drawing a prenuptial agreement, you encourage open communication and may get a better idea of each other's needs and expectations. Also consider drawing up or reviewing your wills at this time.

Some software packages allow you to write your own will and prenuptial agreement, which will save you substantial attorney's fees. However, if you decide to draw either agreement on your own, you should still have an attorney review it.

LEGAL MATTERS

NOTES:

GROOM'S

FORMAL WEAR

You should select your formal wear based on the place, time and formality of your wedding. For a semi-formal or formal wedding, you will need a tuxedo. A tuxedo is the formal jacket worn by men on special or formal occasions. The most popular colors are black, white and gray. Use the following guidelines to select customary attire for your wedding:

Informal
Business suit. White dress shirt and tie.

Semi-formal Daytime
Formal suit. White dress shirt. Cummerbund or vest. Four-in-hand or bow tie.

Semi-formal Evening
Formal suit or dinner jacket. Matching trousers. White shirt. Cummerbund or vest. Black bow tie. Cufflinks and studs.

GROOM'S FORMAL WEAR

Formal Daytime
Cutaway or stroller jacket. Waistcoat. Striped trousers. White wing-Collared shirt. Striped tie. Studs and cufflinks.

Formal Evening
Black dinner jacket. Matching trousers. Waistcoat. White tuxedo shirt. Bow tie. Cummer-bund or vest. Cufflinks.

Very Formal Daytime
Cutaway coat. Wing-collared shirt. Ascot. Striped trousers. Cufflinks. Gloves.

Very Formal Evening
Black tailcoat. Matching striped trousers. Bow tie. White wing-collared shirt. Waistcoat. Patent leather shoes. Studs and cuff-links. Gloves.

In selecting your formal wear, keep in mind the formality and time of day of your wedding, the bride's gown and colors of the bridesmaids' dresses. Consider darker colors for a fall or winter wedding and lighter colors for a spring or summer wedding. When selecting a place to rent your tuxedo, check the reputation of the shop. Make sure they have a wide variety of makes and styles to choose from.

Reserve tuxedos for yourself and your ushers several weeks before the wedding to insure a wide selection and to allow enough time for alterations. Plan to pick up the tuxedos a few days before the wedding to allow time for last minute alterations in case they don't fit properly. Out-of-town men in your wedding party can be sized at any tuxedo shop. They can send their measurements to you or directly to the shop where you are going to rent your tuxedos.

Ask about the store's return policy and be sure you delegate to the appropriate person (usually your best man) the responsibility of returning all tuxedos within the time allotted. Ushers customarily pay for their own tuxedos.

Try to negotiate getting your tuxedo for free or at a discount in exchange for having your father, your fiancée's father and your ushers rent their tuxedos at that shop.

NOTES:

GIFTS

BRIDE'S GIFT

The bride's gift is traditionally given by the groom to the bride. It is typically a personal gift, such as a piece of jewelry.

A string of pearls, a watch, pearl earrings, or a gold chain with a heart-shaped charm holding photos of the two of you are nice options for a bridal gift.

To save money, consider omitting this gift altogether. This gift is not necessary and should be given only if the budget allows it. A pretty card proclaiming your eternal love for your bride is a very special yet inexpensive gift.

USHERS' GIFTS

Ushers' gifts are the gifts given by the groom to his ushers as a permanent keepsake of the wedding.

GIFTS

For ushers' gifts, consider fancy pen sets, wallets, leather belts, silver frames, watches and desk clocks.

Or negotiate with your photographer to take, at no extra charge, professional portraits of each attendant and their escort for use as attendants' gifts. Select a beautiful background, such as your cake table, that will remind your attendants of the occasion. This makes a special yet inexpensive gift for your attendants.

You should deliver your gifts to the ushers at the bachelor party or at the rehearsal dinner. Your gift to the best man may be similar to the ushers' gifts but should be a bit more expensive.

BACHELOR PARTY

The bachelor party is a men-only affair typically organized by your best man. He is responsible for selecting the date and reserving the place and entertainment, as well as inviting your male friends and family. Your best man should also assign responsibilities to your ushers as they should help with the organization of the bachelor party.

You often hear wild stories about bachelor parties being nights full of loose women, alcohol and great fun. However, these stories are actually more rare than you think. Most of the time, they are a big exaggeration of what really happened. It is not uncommon for the guys invited to the bachelor party to create these wild stories and make a vow of never telling the truth about how boring the party really was!

Your typical bachelor party starts with your male friends getting together for dinner and drinking a fair amount of beer. After eating and drinking to their heart's content, they may go bar-hopping.

Your best man should never plan your bachelor party for the night before the wedding, since chances are you will consume a large amount of alcohol and stay up late. You don't want to have a hangover or be exhausted during your wedding. Therefore, it is much more appropriate to have the bachelor party two or three days before the wedding. You should tell your best man that you will be busy the night before the wedding, just in case he is planning to surprise you.

Your best man should designate a driver for you and for those who will drink too much. You don't want to get into an accident days before the wedding or spend your wedding day in jail for drunk driving. Remember, you and your best man are responsible for the well-being of everybody invited to the party.

Whatever you do, make this party a memorable one! Many people do not remember their bachelor party because it was just a typical get-together with friends. Make sure you do something different and enjoy it!

One word of advice: Even though the bachelor party is your last night out as a single man, it does not give you the right to cheat on your fiancée or do something that would upset her. This would be the worst way to begin your married life.

BACHELOR PARTY

NOTES:

_____

_____

_____

_____

_____

_____

_____

_____

_____

_____

_____

_____

_____

_____

_____

_____

_____

_____

_____

_____

_____

_____

REHEARSAL DINNER

The groom's parents customarily host a dinner party following the rehearsal, the evening before the wedding. The dinner usually includes the bridal party, their spouses or guests, both sets of parents, close family members, the officiant, and the wedding consultant and/or coordinator.

The rehearsal dinner can be held just about anywhere, from a restaurant, hotel, or private hall to the groom's parents' home.   Close relatives and out-of-town guests may be included if the budget permits.

Restaurants specializing in Mexican food or pizza are fun yet inexpensive options for a casual rehearsal dinner.

REHEARSAL DINNER

NOTES:

THINGS TO BRING

TO THE REHEARSAL

- Bride's gift (if not already given)
- Marriage license
- Ushers' gifts (if not already given)
- Service providers' fees to give to best man or wedding consultant so s/he can pay them at the wedding

TO THE CEREMONY

- Airline tickets
- Announcements
- Aspirin/Alka Seltzer
- Breath spray/mints
- Bride's ring
- Change of clothes for going away
- Cologne
- Cuff Links

TO THE CEREMONY (CONT.)

- Cummerbund
- Deodorant
- Hair comb
- Hair spray
- Kleenex
- Lint brush
- Luggage
- Neck tie
- Passport
- Shirt
- Shoes
- Socks
- Toothbrush & paste
- Tuxedo
- Underwear

WEDDING FORMATIONS

The following section illustrates the typical ceremony formations (Processional, Recessional and Altar Line Up) for both Christian and Jewish weddings, as well as the typical formations for the Receiving Line, Head Table and Parents' Tables at the reception.

WEDDING FORMATIONS

CHRISTIAN CEREMONY

ℱROCESSIONAL **ℛECESSIONAL**

ABBREVIATIONS

B=Bride
G=Groom
BM=Best Man
MH=Maid of Honor
BF=Bride's Father
BMo=Bride's Mother
O=Officiant

GF=Groom's Father
GM=Groom's Mother
BMa=Bridesmaids
U=Ushers
FG=Flower Girl
RB=Ring Bearer

CHRISTIAN CEREMONY

Altar Line Up

Bride's Pews   Groom's Pews

ABBREVIATIONS

B=Bride   GF=Groom's Father
G=Groom   GM=Groom's Mother
BM=Best Man   BMa=Bridesmaids
MH=Maid of Honor   U=Ushers
BF=Bride's Father   FG=Flower Girl
BMo=Bride's Mother   RB=Ring Bearer
O=Officiant

JEWISH CEREMONY

*P*ROCESSIONAL   *R*ECESSIONAL

ABBREVIATIONS

B=Bride
GM=Groom's Mother
BMa=Bridesmaids
U=Ushers
FG=Flower Girl
RB=Ring Bearer

GF=Groom's Father G=Groom
BM=Best Man
MH=Maid of Honor
BF=Bride's Father
BMo=Bride's Mother
R=Rabbi

JEWISH CEREMONY

Altar Line Up

ABBREVIATIONS

B=Bride
GM=Groom's Mother
BMa=Bridesmaids
U=Ushers
FG=Flower Girl
RB=Ring Bearer

GF=Groom's Father G=Groom
BM=Best Man
MH=Maid of Honor
BF=Bride's Father
BMo=Bride's Mother
R=Rabbi

WEDDING FORMATIONS

ℛECEIVING ℒINE

BMo BF GM GF B G MH BMa BMa BMa

ℋEAD ℐABLE

BMa U BMa BM B G MH U BMa U

ℙARENTS' ℐABLE

BMo
GF   BF
OR
GM
O   OR

ABBREVIATIONS

B=Bride   GF=Groom's Father   G=Groom
BM=Best Man   BMa=Bridesmaids   MH=Maid of Honor
BF=Bride's Father   OR=Other Relatives   BMo=Bride's Mother
O=Officiant   U=Ushers   GM=Groom's Mother

THE WEDDING DAY

Finally, all the months of planning and preparation have come to an end! Your wedding day is supposed to be the happiest day of your life and you should enjoy it. This is the day to forget all arguments or misunderstandings with your fiancée and/or family members.

This is a day to be in a great mood. All attention will be focused on you and your fiancée. If you are in a bad mood or stressed out, hundreds of photographs will reflect that. So this is the time to play politics and smile a lot.

Don't make any other plans for the wedding day. You don't want to be anxious about running out of time or being late to your own wedding. All last-minute errands and chores should be designated to a family member or member of your wedding party.

If you are nervous, ask your best man to help you relax by rubbing your shoulders or telling jokes. Do not drink before the wedding. Nothing gives a worst impression than a tipsy groom or a groom with alcohol on his breath.

Study the list of things to bring to the wedding, found on pages 77-78. If you have not already done so, give your best man the bride's ring as well as the payments to your officiant and other service providers who will need to get paid that day.

Make sure you arrive in plenty of time at the ceremony site. There is nothing that causes more anxiety than being late to your own wedding. Have your best man check with your ushers to make sure they know where to go and at what time to arrive.

This is a day to enjoy and be happy. Remember, the main objective of this day is to marry your fiancée. If something goes wrong, don't let it bother you. Chances are that no one will notice it but yourself.

The best advise we can give you is to relax, loosen up and enjoy your wedding!

TOASTS

It is customary for your best man to offer a toast at the reception to introduce himself, the wedding party, and the newly married couple. This is followed by the groom thanking his best man and then toasting his bride and both sets of parents.

After the groom's toast, anybody else can offer a toast. Typically, the father of the bride and the maid of honor offer a toast.

The toast begins after the receiving line breaks up at a cocktail reception or before dinner during a dinner reception. Toasts can also be offered after the main course or after the cake is served.

Your toast could be to express thanks to everybody involved in planning the wedding, to give thanks to those who traveled long distances to come to your wedding, or to give any other kind of information. It can be serious, such as expressing how much you love your new wife; or it can be funny, such as describing how your fiancée played "hard to get" when you two first met.

Your toast should not be so short that it sounds rude, or so long that your guests get bored. During the toast, everyone rises except those who are being toasted. And no one should drink from their cup until after the toast. After you finish your toast, raise your glass toward the person or persons being toasted.

Your toast should sound sincere and not overly rehearsed. However, it is a good idea to practice it beforehand. If you are anxious about speaking in public, you may want to join your local Toastmaster's Club. This is an organization which helps people develop confidence in public speaking.

DO'S AND DON'TS

Your wedding will last only a few hours but will likely take several months to plan. That is why it is so important to enjoy the complete wedding planning process. This is a time to get excited, to fall even more deeply in love with each other, to learn more about each other, and how to give and take. If you can handle your wedding planning with your fiancée and parents, you can handle anything! Here is a list of do's and don'ts when planning your special day. If you follow these suggestions, your wedding planning will be more enjoyable and the wedding itself will be much more smooth and beautiful.

DO'S

- Read this book completely.

- Hire a professional wedding consultant.

- Maintain a sense of humor.

- Maintain open communication with your fiancée and both sets of parents, especially if they are financing the wedding.

- Be receptive to your parents' ideas, especially if they are financing the wedding.

- Be flexible.

- Keep your overall budget in mind.

- Maintain a regular routine of exercise.

- Eat a well-balanced diet.

- Buy the *Wedding Party Responsibility Cards*, published by Wedding Solutions, and give one to each member of your wedding party.

DO'S (CONT.)

- Read *Easy Wedding Planning*, *Easy Wedding Planning Plus*, or any other of the 16 best selling wedding planning books published by Wedding Solutions.

- Register for gifts; consider a price range that your guests can afford.

- Break-in your shoes well before your wedding day.

- Check recent references for all of your service providers.

- Get everything in writing with your service providers.

- Assign your guests to tables and group them together by age, interest, acquaintances, etc.

- Consider drawing-up a prenuptial agreement and a will.

- Give a rose to each of your mothers as you walk down the aisle during the recessional.

- Try to spend some time with each of your guests and personally thank them for coming to your wedding.

DO'S AND DON'TS

DO'S (CONT.)

- Encourage the bride's parents to introduce their family and friends to the family and friends of the groom's family, and vice-versa.

- Toast both sets of parents at the rehearsal dinner and/or at the reception. Thank them for everything they have done and for giving you a beautiful wedding.

- Eat at the reception, especially if you will be drinking alcohol.

- Keep a smile on your face; there will be many photographs taken of you.

- Preserve the top tier of your wedding cake for your first year anniversary.

- Expect things to go wrong on your wedding day. Most likely something will go wrong, and no one will notice it but yourself. Relax and don't let it bother you.

- Send a special gift to both sets of parents after the wedding, such as a small album. Personalize this gift by having it engraved.

DON'TS

- Don't get involved in other activities; you will be very busy planning your wedding.

- Don't make any major decisions without discussing them openly with your fiancée.

- Don't be controlling. Be open to other people's ideas.

- Don't overspend your budget; this can be extremely stressful.

- Don't wait until the last minute to hire your service providers. The good ones get booked months in advance.

- Don't try to make everybody happy; it is impossible and will make your life miserable.

- Don't try to impress your friends.

- Don't invite old girlfriends to your wedding; you don't want to make your bride feel uncomfortable.

DON'TS (CONT.)

- Don't try to do "everything." Delegate responsibilities to your fiancée, your parents, and to members of your wedding party.

- Don't rely on friends or family to take your wedding photographs. Hire a professional.

- Don't assume that members of your wedding party know what to do. Give each of them a copy of the *Wedding Party Responsibility Cards*, available at most major bookstores.

- Don't assume that your service providers know what to do.

- Don't schedule your bachelor party the night before the wedding. You don't want to have a hangover on your special day.

- Don't arrive late to the ceremony!

- Don't get drunk at your reception; you don't want to make a fool of yourself on your most special day.

- Don't flirt with members of the opposite sex.

DON'TS (CONT.)

- Don't allow your guests to drive drunk after the reception; you may be held responsible.

- Don't rub cake in your bride's face during the cake-cutting ceremony; she may not appreciate it!

- Don't overeat; this may upset your stomach or make you sleepy.

- Don't leave your reception without saying good-bye to your family and friends.

- Don't drive if you have had too much to drink.

DO'S AND DON'TS

NOTES:

THINGS TO DO

DONE	TO DO
❑	
❑	
❑	
❑	
❑	
❑	
❑	
❑	
❑	
❑	
❑	
❑	
❑	
❑	
❑	
❑	

THINGS TO DO

DONE	TO DO
❏	
❏	
❏	
❏	
❏	
❏	
❏	
❏	
❏	
❏	
❏	
❏	
❏	
❏	
❏	
❏	
❏	
❏	
❏	
❏	
❏	

DONE   **TO DO**

- ❏ _____
- ❏ _____
- ❏ _____
- ❏ _____
- ❏ _____
- ❏ _____
- ❏ _____
- ❏ _____
- ❏ _____
- ❏ _____
- ❏ _____
- ❏ _____
- ❏ _____
- ❏ _____
- ❏ _____
- ❏ _____
- ❏ _____
- ❏ _____
- ❏ _____
- ❏ _____
- ❏ _____

THINGS TO DO

DONE   **TO DO**

❏

❏

❏

❏

❏

❏

❏

❏

❏

❏

❏

❏

❏

❏

❏

❏

❏

❏

❏

❏

❏

DONE	TO DO
❑	
❑	
❑	
❑	
❑	
❑	
❑	
❑	
❑	
❑	
❑	
❑	
❑	
❑	
❑	
❑	
❑	
❑	
❑	
❑	

THINGS TO DO

DONE   **TO DO**

❑

❑

❑

❑

❑

❑

❑

❑

❑

❑

❑

❑

❑

❑

❑

❑

❑

❑

❑

❑

❑

THE ULTIMATE
Honeymoon
Planner

A COMPREHENSIVE GUIDE
CONTAINING ALL THE INFORMATION A
GROOM SHOULD KNOW WHEN
PLANNING A HONEYMOON

CONTENTS

INTRODUCTION 107

TYPES OF HONEYMOONS................................. 109

    Traditional Honeymoons..................................... 110

    Non-Traditional Honeymoons........................... 115

CHOOSING YOUR DESTINATION 117

CREATING A WISH LIST..................................... 119

HELPFUL RESOURCES 131

CREATING A BUDGET 155

TIPPING GUIDE 169

THINGS TO PACK 173

PACKING CHECKLIST... 175

CONTENTS

INTERNATIONAL TRAVEL 183

    Passports and Visas 183

    Health Concerns 190

    Customs... 192

THINGS TO DO CHECKLIST 195

INTRODUCTION

Your honeymoon is the time to celebrate your new life together as a married couple. It should be the vacation of a lifetime. This does not necessarily mean spending your life's earnings, but the vacation should reflect the special interests you share as a couple.

The honeymoon is traditionally the groom's responsibility. However, the planning of your honeymoon should be a joint decision as to where to go, how long to stay and how much money to spend.

You will find many tools and suggestions on the following pages to help you plan this important trip. After reading this book, you will have information on different types of honeymoons, and you should be able to determine the perfect honeymoon destination, research and select a responsible travel agent, gather useful information using the resource leads provided, establish a reasonable budget with confidence, and - most importantly - walk away with the assurance that you are planning the honeymoon of a lifetime! Start planning your honeymoon months before the wedding. Many locations that are popular with honeymooners tend to book fairly quickly, so the earlier you plan your trip, the better values you'll usually find.

There are many choices to make and many plans to be made but most of them seem to fall into place once you've made the toughest decision... where to go.

Many people have a preconceived notion of where a honeymoon should take place. And indeed, these locations are, year after year, some of the places most frequently visited by newlyweds. We'll take a look at some of these "traditional" destinations as well as some that are a little "less traditional."

Think about what you and your fiancée might find appealing (and unappealing) in the following honeymoon vacations. Be careful not to assume what your new bride may be looking for in a honeymoon. Couples are often surprised when they discover what the other partner considers a "vacation." Refer to the section entitled "Choosing a Destination" to determine what each other's ideal vacation includes.

TYPES OF

HONEYMOONS

Listed on the following pages are sample honeymoon plans -- both traditional and non-traditional. A brief description of some of the most popular honeymoon trips (ones that have remained popular with newlyweds for generations) is provided as well.

You can get very helpful information on planning a vacation package in the following brochures from the United States Tour Operator Association, (212) 599-6599.
URL: www.ustoa.com.

- How to Select a Tour Vacation Package
- Worldwide Tour and Vacation Package Finder
- The Standard for Confident Travel

TRADITIONAL HONEYMOONS

Cruises

Cruises are a popular retreat for those who want the luxury of a hospitable resort with the added benefit of visiting one or more new areas. There are hundreds of different cruise options available to you. Typically, almost everything is included in the cost of your cruise: extravagant dining, unlimited group and individual activities, relaxing days and lively nights.

Costs vary greatly depending on the location the cruise will visit (if any) and your cabin accommodations. Locations range from traveling the Mississippi River to encircling the Greek Isles. Spend some time choosing your cabin. Most of them are small, but pay attention to distracting things, such as noisy areas and busy pathways, that might be located close by. Even though most everything is included in your cost, be sure to ask and clarify which items may or may not be included.

Even though most everything is included in your cost, be sure to ask about those items which may not be included (alcoholic beverages, sundries, spa treatments and tips generally are not included.) Request a helpful publication entitled Answers to Your Most Frequently Asked Questions, published by Cruise Lines International Association, (212) 921-0066, www.cruising.org.

All Inclusive Resorts

Many newlyweds, tired from the previous months of wedding planning and accompanying stress, opt for the worry-free guarantee of an all-inclusive resort. Some resorts are for the entire family, some are for couples only (not necessarily newlywed), and some are strictly for honeymooners. Most of these resorts are nestled on a picturesque island beach catering to your relaxation needs.

Most offer numerous sports, water activities, entertainment, and exceptional service and attention. Your costs will vary depending on the location you choose, and there are many, many to choose from. "All-inclusive" means everything is included in your price. You won't have to worry about meals, drinks, tour fees or even tips.

One way of considering if this is a good option for you is to list all of the activities that the vacation package offers that you are interested in. Add up the individual costs and compare. If you wouldn't be participating much in the activities, food, and drink, you may actually save money by arranging your own trip at an independent resort. Even still, many couples prefer to spend the extra money in exchange for a vacation free of planning and wearying decisions.

Because of its convenience, many couples choose this resort option as the setting for their honeymoon. Sandals Resorts and Spas are some of the most popular all-inclusive locations.

The Poconos

The Poconos Honeymoon resorts are located in Pennsylvania and are considered to be some of the most popular honeymoon destinations around. The Poconos offer a variety of individual resorts, each heavily laden with fanciful symbols of romance and sweet desires. The atmosphere is perfect for those who want to be enveloped in a surrounding where you'll never forget you're in love and on your honeymoon. Some travel packages here are considered all-inclusive, but as always, be sure to ask about exclusions and extras. For information about honeymooning in the Poconos, call 1-800- POCONOS.

Walt Disney World

Another popular destination for those seeking a "theme" resort are those offered as Disney's Fairy Tale Honeymoons. These vacation packages include accommodations at Disney's exclusive resorts and admission to their theme parks. Some packages are also available with accommodations at some of the privately owned resorts at Disney World. Prices for Disney packages can range greatly depending on your tastes and the amount of activity you desire. For information on Disney's honeymoon packages, call (407) 828-3400 or visit them online at www.disney weddings.com.

Inquire with your travel agent about day or overnight cruises leaving from nearby ports in Florida. This is one way to combine two very popular honeymoon options into one!

TYPES OF HONEYMOONS

Other popular and traditional honeymoon plans are:

- Enjoying the beaches and unique treasures of the Hawaiian islands

- Exploring Northern California's romantic wine country

- Ski and snowboard package getaways in Vermont, New Hampshire, Colorado, and Northern California

NON-TRADITIONAL HONEYMOONS

- Bicycling in Nova Scotia while relaxing at quaint bed and breakfast Inns

- Participating in a white water river rafting expedition

- Mingling with the owners and fellow guests on a Wild West Dude Ranch

- Visiting landmarks and parks while enjoying the convenience of a traveling home in a rented RV

- Mustering up the courage and stamina for an aggressive hiking tour of the Canadian Rockies

- Training for and participating in a dog sled race in the brisk tundra of Alaska

- "Roughing it" while enjoying the splendor of a safari in East Africa

TYPES OF HONEYMOONS

NOTES:

CHOOSING YOUR

DESTINATION

Maybe your idea of a perfect honeymoon is ten days of adventure and discovery; but for your fiancée, it may be ten days of resting in a beach chair with romantic strolls in the evening. The choices for honeymoon vacations are as varied as brides and grooms themselves. Deciding together on a honeymoon destination is a wonderful opportunity to discover more about each other and negotiate a vacation that will leave both of you relaxed, fulfilled and even more in love.

First, determine the type of atmosphere and climate you prefer. Then consider the types of activities you would like to engage in.

Do you want the weather to be hot for swimming at the beach... or warm for long guided tours of unknown cities... or cooler for day-long hikes in the woods... or cold for optimum skiing conditions? Keep in mind the time of year in which your wedding falls. Will you be escaping from extreme temperatures?

If you have a specific destination in mind, you (or your travel agent) will need to do some research to be sure the weather conditions will be suitable for your planned activities.

Review the previous chapters on traditional and non-traditional honeymoons and note what you feel are the pros and cons of each type of vacation. The two of you should have lots of images and possibilities in your mind at this point! The next step is to determine the most perfect atmosphere to provide the setting for your honeymoon. The following sections, "Creating A Wish List" and "Helpful Resources," will guide you through this next step and beyond.

CREATING A

WISH LIST

Together with your fiancée, complete the following wish list worksheet. You should each check off your preferences even if both of you don't agree on them. There are many locations that provide a variety of activities. Remember, you don't need to spend every minute of your honeymoon together, but your honeymoon destination should be one that intrigues both of you.

This worksheet is divided into 5 sections. You will be considering location, accommodations, meals, activities, and nightlife. While completing the worksheet, be as true to your interests as possible; don't concern yourself with finances and practicality at this point. This is your chance to let your mind wander! Think about what you would like to fill your days and nights with. This is the honeymoon of your dreams...

You step out of the plane, train, car or boat that took you to your honeymoon destination. You sigh with satisfaction

CREATING A WISH LIST

at the memory of your flawless and enjoyable wedding as your feet touch the ground...

... What type of overall atmosphere do you see yourself stepping into? What is the weather like?

... Do you picture a long stretch of beach, towering mountains, blossoming vineyards or city skyscrapers? Is the dry sand of the desert blowing or is everything captured under glistening snowcaps?

... Are there many people walking around (many locals, many tourists), or is it a secluded retreat?

... Are you relaxing indoors in a resort with a pampering environment that caters to your comfort, or do you return to a simple, modest hotel or motel after a long day of sightseeing, touring and dining? Are you camping in the middle of your activities--hiking, climbing, fishing, etc.?

... Do you see yourself interacting much with others? Would you like to have these activities be organized? Are there vistas and horizons to gaze endlessly upon, or is there an abundance of visual activity and changing scenery?

... Are you enjoying exotic foods elaborately displayed and available to you at your leisure? Are you testing out your sense of adventure on the local cuisine and dining hot spots? Are you eating fast foods and pizza in exchange for spending your time and money on other items and activities that make your vacation exciting?

... Are your evenings filled with romantic strolls or festivities that run late into the night? Are you staying in for romantic evenings or re-energizing for another busy day of honeymooning?

HOW TO USE THIS WORKSHEET

Each of you separately should place a check mark next to the items or images on the wish list that appeal to you. After you have finished, highlight those items that both of you feel are important (the items that were checked by both of you).

Next, each of you should highlight, in a different colored marker or pen, 2-3 items in each category that you feel are very important to you individually (even though the other person may not have checked it.)

CREATING A WISH LIST

Bride	Groom	LOCATION
❑	❑	Hot Weather
❑	❑	Mild Weather
❑	❑	Cold Weather
❑	❑	Dry Climate
❑	❑	Moist Climate
❑	❑	Sand and Beaches
❑	❑	Lakes/Ponds
❑	❑	Wilderness/Wooded Area
❑	❑	Mountains
❑	❑	Fields
❑	❑	City Streets
❑	❑	Small Local Town
❑	❑	Large Metropolitan Area
❑	❑	Popular Tourist Destination
❑	❑	Visiting Among the Locals
❑	❑	Nighttime Weather Conducive to Outdoor Activities

Bride	Groom	**LOCATION** (CONT.)
❑	❑	Nighttime Weather Conducive to Indoor Activities
❑	❑	"Modern" Resources & Service
❑	❑	"Roughing It" On Your Own
❑	❑	Culture and Customs You Are Familiar and Comfortable With
❑	❑	New Cultures and Customs You Would Like to Get to Know

Bride	Groom	**ACCOMMODATIONS**
❑	❑	Part of a Larger Resort Community
❑	❑	A Stand Alone Building
❑	❑	Lodging Amongst Other Fellow Tourists
❑	❑	Lodging Amongst Couples Only
❑	❑	Lodging Amongst Fellow Newlyweds Only

CREATING A WISH LIST

Bride	Groom	ACCOMMODATIONS (CONT.)
❑	❑	Lodging Amongst Locals
❑	❑	Large Room or Suite
❑	❑	Plush, Highly Decorated Surroundings
❑	❑	Modestly Sized Room
❑	❑	Modest Décor
❑	❑	Balcony
❑	❑	Private Jacuzzi in Room
❑	❑	Room Service
❑	❑	Chamber Maid Service
❑	❑	Laundry/Dry Cleaning Service Available
❑	❑	Laundry Room Available
❑	❑	Beauty Salon on Premises
❑	❑	Gym on Premises
❑	❑	Gift Shop on Premises
❑	❑	Pool on Premises

Bride	Groom	ACCOMMODATIONS (CONT.)
❏	❏	Poolside Bar Service
❏	❏	Sauna, Hot Tub on Premises
❏	❏	Common Gathering Lounge for Guests

Bride	Groom	MEALS
❏	❏	Casual Dining
❏	❏	Formal Dining
❏	❏	Prepared by Executive Chefs
❏	❏	Prepared by Yourself/Grocery Store
❏	❏	Variety of Local and Regional Cuisine
❏	❏	Traditional American Cuisine
❏	❏	Opportunity for Picnics
❏	❏	Exotic, International Menu
❏	❏	Entertainment While Dining
❏	❏	Planned Meal Times

Bride	Groom	MEALS (CONT.)
❑	❑	Dining Based on Your Own Schedule
❑	❑	Fast Food Restaurants
❑	❑	Vegetarian/Special Diet Meals
❑	❑	Delis, Diners

Bride	Groom	ACTIVITIES
❑	❑	Sun Bathing
❑	❑	Snorkeling
❑	❑	Diving
❑	❑	Swimming
❑	❑	Jet Skiing
❑	❑	Water Skiing
❑	❑	Fishing
❑	❑	Sailing
❑	❑	Snow Skiing
❑	❑	Snow Boarding

Bride	Groom	ACTIVITIES (CONT.)
❏	❏	Hiking/Rock Climbing
❏	❏	Camping
❏	❏	Golf
❏	❏	Tennis
❏	❏	Aerobics
❏	❏	Site-Seeing Suggestions and Guidance
❏	❏	Planned Bus/Guided Tours
❏	❏	Ability to Go Off on Your Own
❏	❏	Historic Tours
❏	❏	Art Museums
❏	❏	Theater
❏	❏	Exploring Family Heritage

CREATING A WISH LIST

Bride	Groom	OTHER IMPORTANT ELEMENTS
❏	❏	
❏	❏	
❏	❏	
❏	❏	
❏	❏	
❏	❏	
❏	❏	
❏	❏	
❏	❏	
❏	❏	
❏	❏	
❏	❏	
❏	❏	
❏	❏	
❏	❏	
❏	❏	
❏	❏	
❏	❏	
❏	❏	
❏	❏	
❏	❏	

Your wish lists, at this point, probably look like a list of all of the positive elements of all of your dream vacations combined. List as many things as you can think of. The more information you have, the better the suggestions your travel agent (or yourself if you'll be doing your own research) will be able to make.

Together, using this wish list, you will discover a honeymoon destination and match a honeymoon style that will fulfill your dreams.

The resource leads and exercises provided in the rest of this book will help you get from wish list to reality. Happy planning!

CREATING A WISH LIST

NOTES:

_____

_____

_____

_____

_____

_____

_____

_____

_____

_____

_____

_____

_____

_____

_____

_____

_____

_____

_____

_____

_____

_____

HELPFUL RESOURCES

The following pages include helpful resources that will come in handy when planning your honeymoon. Find information regarding travel agents, guide books, websites, and telephone numbers of travel bureaus from around the world.

TRAVEL AGENTS

Hiring the services of a good travel agent will take a lot of unnecessary pressure off of you. In the past, you may have felt you did not need the assistance of a travel agent when planning a vacation. Planning a honeymoon, however, can often be far more involved and stressful than a "regular" vacation, due to the simple fact that you are also deeply enmeshed in the planning of your wedding!

Therefore, you should take advantage of the professional resources available to you when working out the small details and finding the best values. Keep in mind, though, that you will still probably want to do some research on your own, ask for second opinions, and most of all, read the fine print.

Since a travel agent can become one of your most valuable resources, you will want to consider a few important things when trying to select one. Ask family, friends, and coworkers for personal recommendations (especially from former honeymooners). If you are unable to find an agent through a personal referral, then select a few agencies that are established nearby (from newspapers, phone books, etc.)

Next, you will want to make an appointment with an agent or speak to one over the phone. Pay close attention to the following items in bold and then make your decision.

Find out if they are a member of the American Society of Travel Agents (ASTA). Additionally, find out if they are also a Certified Travel Counselor (CTC), or possibly a Destination Specialist (DS).

ASTA: Members of this organization are required to have at least 5 years travel agent experience. They also agree to adhere to strict codes and standards of integrity in travel issues as established by the national society. In most states, there are no formal regulations requiring certain qualifications for being a travel agent. In other words, any person can decide to call him/herself a travel agent.

CTC: Certified Travel Counselors have successfully completed a 2 year program in travel management.

DS: Destination Specialists have successfully completed studies focusing on a particular region of travel.

For a list of **ASTA** agencies in your area, call or write:

American Society of Travel Agents
Consumer Affairs Department
1101 King Street, Suite 200
Alexandria, VA 22314
(703) 739-2782
www.ASTAnet.com

For a list of Destination Specialists and Certified Travel Agents in your area, call or write:

Institute of Certified Travel Agents
148 Linden Street
P.O. Box 56

Wellesley, MA 02181
(800) 542-4282 (press "0" to be connected to a Travel
Counselor)
www.ICTA.com

QUESTIONS TO QUALIFY YOUR TRAVEL AGENT:

- How long has the Travel Agency been in business?

- How long has the Travel Agent been with the agency?

- How much experience does the Travel Agent have?
  Any special studies or travels?

- Do they have a good resource library?

- Does the agent/agency have a variety of brochures
  to offer?

- Do they have video tapes to lend?

- Do they have a recommended reading list of travel
  aid books?

- Does the agent seem to understand your responses on your wish list and budget?

- Does he/she seem excited to help you?

- Does the agent listen carefully to your ideas? Take notes on your conversations? Ask you questions to ensure a full understanding?

- Is the agent able to offer a variety of different possibilities that suit your interests based on your wish list? Do the suggestions fall within your budget?

- Can the agent relay back to you (in his/her own words) what your wish list priorities are? What your budget priorities are?

- Is the agent prompt in getting back in touch with you?

- Is the agent reasonably quick in coming up with suggestions and alternatives? Are the suggestions exciting and within reason?

- Does the agent take notes on your interests (degree of sports, leisure, food, etc.)?

- Does the travel agency provide a 24-hour emergency help line?

- Are you documenting your conversations and getting all of your travel plans and reservations confirmed in writing?

Aside from just offering information and arrangements about locations and discounts, a good travel agent should also provide you with information about passports, customs, travel and health insurance, travelers' checks, and any other information important to a traveler.

OTHER SOURCES

National bridal magazines and general travel magazines are a great place to search for honeymoon ideas. But remember, you cannot always believe every word in paid advertising.

In addition to the information your travel agent provides, you can also obtain maps, brochures and other useful items on your own. At the end of this section, you will find many useful phone numbers to help you in contacting tourist bureaus and travel agencies worldwide. These offices are extremely helpful in acquiring both general information (about weather, tourist attractions, landmarks, and even coupons or promotional brochures "selling" the area) and more specific information about reputable hotels, inns, bed and breakfasts, restaurants, etc.

Also provided in this section are phone numbers for sources specializing in information about traveling by train (in the United States as well as abroad) and for camping and hiking throughout the country.

If you have Internet access you can acquire volumes and volumes of information and titillating pictures about your possible destinations. You can even "chat" with fellow soon-to-be honeymooners or recent honeymooners about their experiences.

If you don't currently have internet access, local libraries often provide limited free time and user-assistance for their members.

Your local library, the travel section of book stores, and travel stores are also excellent sources for finding information and tips relevant to your travel needs. You will find books on traveling in general as well as books specific to the region or destination you will be visiting. There are numerous tour books, maps, language books and tapes, as well as books about a location's culture, traditions, customs, climate and geography.

These books are a great source of information since they are independent from the locations they describe and are therefore impartial, objective, and usually contain correct, unbiased information. You can also find books and other resources describing (and sometimes rating) restaurants, hotels, shows and tours. Books on bargain hunting and finding the best deals are common as well.

SOURCES TO READ

- *The Ultimate Guide to the World's Best Wedding and Honeymoon Destinations*, written by Elizabeth & Alex Lluch. A comprehensive resource for planning your honeymoon, including information on popular destinations and information on hotels and resorts.

- The Stephen Birnbaum Travel Guides

- Frommer's Guides

- Michelin's Green Guides; Michelin's Red Guides

- Insight Guides

- Let's Go! guides

- Fodor's Guides

- Fielding Travel Books

- AYH Handbook and Hosteler's Manual: Europe and the United States

- The New York Times Practical Traveler

- Mobil Travel Guide

BACKGROUND NOTES

- U.S. Government notes containing information about the culture, people, geography, history, government, economy, and maps of most countries worldwide.

  The U.S. Government Printing Office Cost: $1.00
  (202) 512-1800, or download at: www.access.gpo.gov

- National Park Service publications:
  (202) 208-4747
  www.nps.gov

- National Park System Map and Guide

- The National Parks: Index

- National Forest Service publications:
  (202) 205-8333
  A Guide to Your National Forests
  www.fs.fed.us

HELPFUL RESOURCES

STATE TOURISM BUREAUS

Alabama Bureau of Tourism
        800-ALABAMA .... www.touralabama.com
Alaska Travel Industry Association
        907-929-2200 .... www.travelalaska.com
Arizona Office of Tourism
        866-275-5816 .... www.arizonaguide.com
Arkansas Dept. of Parks and Tourism
        800-NATURAL .... www.arkansas.com
California Tourism Office
        800-862-2543 .... www.gocalif.com
Colorado Tourism Board
        800-COLORADO .... www.colorado.com
Connecticut Vacation Center
        800-CT-BOUND .... www.ctbound.com
D.C. Convention and Visitors Association
        202-789-7000 .... www.washington.org
Delaware Tourism Office
        866-284-7483 .... www.visitdelaware.com
Visit Florida
        850-488-5607 .... www.flausa.com
Georgia Department of Industry Trade
        800-VISIT-GA .... www.georgia.org
Hawaii Visitors & Convention Bureau
        800-464-2924 .... www.hawaii.com
Idaho Division of Tourism Development
        800-635-7820 .... www.visitid.org

STATE TOURISM BUREAUS (CONT.)

Illinois Bureau of Tourism
    800-2-CONNECT .... www.enjoyillinois.com
Indiana Department of Commerce
    888-ENJOY-IN ....www.enjoyindiana.com
Iowa Tourism Office
    888-472-6035 ....www.traveliowa.com
Kansas Department of Travel & Tourism
    800-2-KANSAS ....www.travelks.com
Kentucky Dept. of Travel Development
    800-225-TRIP ....www.kentuckytourism.com
Louisiana Office of Tourism
    800-33-GUMBO ....www.louisianatravel.com
Maine Bureau of Tourism
    888-624-6345 ....www.visitmaine.com
Maryland Office of Tourist Development
    800-MD-IS-FUN..............................www.mdisfun.org
Massachusetts Department of Tourism
    800-447-MASS ....www.massvacation.com
Michigan Department of Commerce
    888-78-GREAT..............................www.michigan.org
Minnesota Office of Tourism
    800-657-3700 ....www.exploreminnesota.com
Mississippi Office of Tourism
    800-WARMEST ....www.visitmississippi.org
Missouri Travel Center
    800-877-1234..................................www.visitmo.com

HELPFUL RESOURCES

STATE TOURISM BUREAUS (CONT.)

Montana Travel Promotion Division
       800-VISIT-MT..................................www.visitmt.com
Nebraska Dept. of Travel and Tourism
       800-228-4307..........................www.visitnebraska.org
Nevada Commission on Tourism
       800-NEVADA-8......................www.travelnevada.com
New Hampshire Division of Tourism
       800-FUN-IN-NH..............................www.visitnh.gov
New Jersey Office of Travel & Tourism
       800-JERSEY-7.....................................www.visitnj.org
New Mexico Department of Tourism
       800-SEE-NEWMEX..................www.newmexico.org
New York Division of Tourism
       800-CALL-NYS.....................www.www.iloveny.com
North Carolina Travel & Tourism Division
       800-VISIT-NC...................................www.visitnc.com
North Dakota Tourism Division
       800-HELLO-ND........................www.ndtourism.com
Ohio Department of Travel & Tourism
       800-BUCKEYE.......................www.ohiotourism.com
Oklahoma Tourism and Recreation Dept.
       800-652-6552...............................www.travelok.com
Oregon Tourism Commission
       800-547-7842........................www.traveloregon.com
Pennsylvania Department of Tourism
       800-VISIT-PA...........................www.experiencepa.com

STATE TOURISM BUREAUS (CONT.)

Rhode Island Tourism Division
        800-556-2484 ....www.visitrhodeisland.com
South Carolina Dept. of Parks, Rec. and Tourism
        800-346-3634 ....www.discoversouthcarolina.com
South Dakota Division of Tourism
        800-S-DAKOTA ....www.travelsd.com
Tennessee Department of Tourism
        800-GO-2-1ENN ....www.tnvacation.com
Texas Travel and Information Bureau
        800-888-8-TEX ....www.traveltex.com
Utah Travel Council
        800-200-1160 ....www.utah.com
Vermont Travel Division
        800-VERMONT..................www.travel-vermont.com
Virginia Division of Tourism
        800-VISIT-VA ....www.virginia.org
Washington Tourism Development
        800-544-1800 ....www.experiencewashington.com
West Virginia Div. of Tourism & Parks
        800-CALL-WVA ....www.callwva.com
Wisconsin Division of Tourism
        800-432-TRIP ....www.travelwisconsin.com
Wyoming Travel & Tourism
        800-CALL-WYO ....www.wyomingtourism.org

STATE TOURISM BUREAUS (CONT.)

U.S. Virgin Islands Division of Tourism
    800-372-USVI ....www.usvitourism.vi

INTERNATIONAL TOURISM BUREAUS

Anguilla Tourist Information
    800-553-4939 ....www.anguilla-vacation.com
Antigua Tourist Office
    212-541-4117 ....www.antigua-barbuda.org
Argentina Tourist Information
    800-722-5737 ......www.turismo.gov.ar/eng/menu.htm
Aruba Tourism Authority
    404-89-ARUBA ....www.aruba.com
Australian Tourist Commission
    ı61 2 9360 1111 ....www.australia.com
Austrian National Tourist Office
    212-944-6880 ....www.austria-tourism.at
Bahamas Tourist Office
    800-422-4262 ....www.bahamas.com
Balkan Holidays
    800-822-1106 ....www.balkan-travel.com
Barbados Board of Tourism
    800-221-9831 ....www.barbados.org

INTERNATIONAL TOURISM BUREAUS (CONT.)

Belgian Tourist Office
212-758-8130 ....www.visitbelgium.com
Belize Tourist Board
800-624-0686 ....travelbelize.org
Bermuda Department of Tourism
800-BERMUDA ....www.bermudatourism.com
Bonaire Tourist Information Office
00-BONAIRE ....www.infobonaire.com
Brazil Tourism Office
800-544-5503 ....www.brazilres.com
Visit Britain
800-462-2748 .... www.travelbritain.org
Canadian Consulate
613-946-1000 ....www.travelcanada.ca
Alberta
800-661-8888 ....www.travelalberta.com
British Columbia
800-HELLO-BC ....www.hellobc.com
Manitoba
800-665-0040 ....www.travelmanitoba.com
New Brunswick
800-561-0123..............www.tourismnewbrunswick.ca
Newfoundland
800-563-6353 ....www.gov.nf.ca/tourism/

INTERNATIONAL TOURISM BUREAUS (CONT.)

Nova Scotia
    800-565-0000 ....www.explorens.com
Ontario
    800-ONTARIO ....www.ontariotravel.net
Prince Edward
    800-PEI-PLAY..................................www.peiplay.com
Quebec
    877-BONJOUR ....www.bonjourquebec.com
Saskatchewan
    877-2-ESCAPE ....www.sasktourism.com
Yukon
    867-667-5340 ....www.touryukon.com
Caribbean Tourism Organization
    800-603-3545.......................www.doitcaribbean.com
Cayman Islands Department of Tourism
    212-889-9009 ....www.caymanislands.ky
Chile National Tourist Board
    800-244-5366 ....www.visitchile.com
China National Tourist Office
    818-545-7505..www.cnto.org
Colombian Consulate
    202-332-7476 ....www.colombiaemb.org
Cook Islands Tourist Authority
    888-994-2665..........................www.cook-islands.com

INTERNATIONAL TOURISM BUREAUS (CONT.)

Costa Rican Tourist Board
    800-343-6332 ....www.visitcostarica.com
Curacao Tourist Board
    800-683-7660...................www.curacao-tourism.com
Cyprus Consulate General
    212-683-5280 ....www.cyprustourism.org
CEDOK (Czech Republic and Slovakia)
    212-288-0830...........................www.czechcenter.com
Denmark Tourist Board
    212-885-9700 ....www.visitdenmark.com
Dominican Republic Tourist Info. Center
    888-DR-INFO ....www.dominica.com.do
Egyptian Tourist Authority
    312-280-4666 ....touregypt.net
Fiji Visitors Bureau
    800-YEA-FIJI...................................www.BulaFiji.com
Finland Tourist Board
    800-FIN-INFO ....www.gofinland.org
French Government Tourist Office
    410-286-8310 ....www.franceguide.com
French West Indies
    877-956-1234 ....www.franceguide.com
German National Tourist Office
    323-655-6085 ....www.visits-to-germany.com

INTERNATIONAL TOURISM BUREAUS (CONT.)

Greece National Tourist Authority
212-421-5777 ....www.greektourism.com
Grenada Department of Tourism
212-687-9554 ....www.grenada.org
Guam Visitors Bureau
800-US-3-GUAM ....www.visitguam.org
Guatemala Tourist Commission
888-464-8281 ....www.guatemala.travel.com.gt
Honduras Tourist Bureau
800-410-9608 ....www.honduras.com
Hong Kong Tourist Association
212-421-3382 ....www.discoverhongkong.com/usa/
Hungary Tourist Board
212-355-0240..........................www.gotohungary.com
Iceland Tourist Board
212-885-9747 ....www.icetourist.is
India Tourist Office
800-953-9399 ....www.tourismindia.com
Indonesian Tourist Office
808-638-8500 ....www.indonesia2001.com
Ireland Tourist Board
800-223-6470 ....www.tourismireland.com
Israeli Government Tourist Office
888-77-ISRAEL ....www.goisrael.com

HELPFUL RESOURCES   149

INTERNATIONAL TOURISM BUREAUS (CONT.)

Italian Tourist Office
    212-245-4822 ....www.italiantourism.com
Jamaican Tourist Board
    800-JAMAICA ....www.jamaicatravel.com
Japan National Tourist Office
    212-757-5640 ....www.japantravelinfo.com
Kenya Tourist Office
    202-387-6101.......................www.magicalkenya.com
Korea National Tourist Office
    800-868-7567...........................www.tour2korea.com
Luxembourg National Tourist Office
    212-935-8888....................www.visitluxembourg.com
Macau Tourist Office
    (853) 333000 ....www.macautourism.gov.mo
Malaysian Tourist Centre
    213-689-970 ....www.tourismmalaysia.com
Malta National Tourist Office
    212-430-3799.............................www.visitmalta.com
Mexican Tourist Office
    800-44-MEXICO ....www.visitmexico.com
Monaco Government Tourist Office
    800-753-9696 ....www.visitmonaco.com
Morocco National Tourist Office
    407-827-5337 ....wwww.tourism-in-morocco.com

INTERNATIONAL TOURISM BUREAUS (CONT.)

Netherlands Board of Tourism
        416-363-1577 ....www.goholland.com
New Zealand Tourist Office
        800-NEW-ZEALAND ....www.newzealand.com
Norway Scandinavia Tourist Offices
        212-421-7333 ....www.norway.org
Papua/New Guinea Tourist Office
        949-752-5440........................www.pngtourism.org.pg
Philippine Department of Tourism
        213-487-4525 ....wowphilippines.com.ph
Poland National Tourism Office
        201-420-3370 ....www.polandtour.org
Portugal National Tourist Office
        212-354-4403 ....www.portugal.org
Puerto Rico Tourism Office
        800-866-STAR....................www.gotopuertorico.com,
Romanian National Tourist Office
        212-545-8484 ....www.romaniatourism.com
Russian Travel Information Office
        877-221-7120 ....www.russia-travel.com
Singapore Tourist Board
        323-852-1901........................www.singapore-usa.com
South African Tourism Board
        800-822-5368 ....www.satour.org

INTERNATIONAL TOURISM BUREAUS (CONT.)

Spain National Tourism Office
    212-265-8822 ....www.okspain.org
Sri Lanka Tourist Board
    202-483-4025 ....www.slembassyusa.org
St. Kitts Tourist Board
    212-535-1234 ....www.stkittsnevis.org
St. Lucia Tourist Board
    800-4-ST-LUCIA ....www.stlucia.org
St. Maarten Tourist Office
    800-786-2278 ....www.st-maarten.com
St. Vincent/Grenadines Tourist Office
    212-687-4981 ....www.svgtourism.com
Sweden Travel & Tourism Board
    212-885-9700 ....www.visit-sweden.com
Switzerland National Tourist Office
    877-SWITZERLAND ....www.myswitzerland.com
Tahitian Tourist Board
    310-414-8484 ....www.tahiti-tourisme.com
Taiwan Visitors Association
    212-867-1632 ....www.taiwan.net.tw
Thailand Tourism Authority
    212-432-0433......................www.tourismthailand.org
Trinidad and Tobago Tourist Board
    868-675-7034 ....www.visitTNT.com

INTERNATIONAL TOURISM BUREAUS (CONT.)

Tunisian Tourist Office
202-862-1850 ....www.tourismtunisia.com
Turkish Tourism Office
212-687-2194 ....www.tourismturkey.org
Venezuela Tourism Association
415-331-0100 ....www.venezuela.com

OTHER TOURISM BUREAUS AND SERVICES

National Park Service
202-208-4747 ....www.nps.gov
American Automobile Association
407-444-8000..www.aaa.com
Amtrak National Railroad Passenger Info.
800-872 7245 ....www.amtrak.com
Rail Europe
800-438-7245 ....www.raileurope.com
Via Rail Canada
800-561-3949 ....www.viarail.ca

NOTES:

CREATING A BUDGET

You want your honeymoon to give you luxurious experiences and priceless memories. But you don't want to return from your vacation faced with debts and unnecessary feelings of guilt for not having stayed within a reasonable budget.

This should be the vacation of a lifetime. You can make this trip into anything your imagination allows. Pay attention to which experiences or details you would consider a "must have" and prioritize from there. As you work with your budget, stay focused on those top priority items and allow less "elaborate" solutions for lower priority items. If you stay true to your most important vacation objectives, the minor sacrifices along the way will barely be noticed.

Perhaps, at this point, you don't know how many days your honeymoon will last. Often, the number of days you'll vacation depends on the type of honeymoon you choose. If you (and your travel agent) are designing your own honeymoon, the typical cost-per-day will most likely determine your

CREATING A BUDGET

length of stay. If you opt for a cruise or another type of pre-arranged vacation, your length of stay will probably be dependent upon the designated length of the travel package. By determining a basic, overall budget at the start, you will know what your limits are.

Yes, this is a very romantic time... but try to remain realistic! Once you have an idea of your spending limits, your choices will be much easier to make.

Don't be discouraged if you're unable to spend an infinite amount of money on this trip. Very few couples are able to live life so carefree. You can still experience a honeymoon that will leave you filled with those priceless memories... it's all in the planning!

The following budget worksheets will help guide you in creating your honeymoon budget. You may want to make copies of this worksheet so that you can create several budget plans. Keep trying different variations until you are satisfied with how your expenses will be allocated. When comparing your potential honeymoon options, you'll find that laying out a simple budget is an effective and essential tool for making decisions.

CREATING A BUDGET

GENERAL BUDGET

Traditionally, the groom is responsible for the honeymoon. The groom will take on the challenges of gathering information and working through the necessary details of providing a perfect honeymoon for his new bride... and himself! Nowadays, many couples find it necessary for both the bride and groom to contribute to the cost in order to experience the honeymoon of their dreams. (Today, the average newlywed couple spends $3,500-$5,000 on their honeymoon.) Many couples, together, determine what each partner will contribute and then shape the budget from there.

Some couples find that including the suggestion of a "Money Contribution towards a Memorable Honeymoon" as a gift in their bridal registry is a great way for friends and family to contribute to the trip. Some couples also include some version of a "Dollar Dance" at their reception. This is a great way for the bride and groom to dance with many of their guests while accepting the dollar "dance fee" as a contribution to their honeymoon. Some couples choose to pursue other options for building up the honeymoon savings... part time jobs, yard sales, etc.

Whatever your methods may be, remember that increasing

the amount of money you will spend does not automatically ensure a more pleasurable and enjoyable vacation. Your most important and effective resource is your commitment to planning. You will see that, regardless of what your budget limits may be, your vacation possibilities are endless.

Note: Even if you think you have a good sense of what you will spend (or even if you plan on going with an all-inclusive package) going through this exercise is a smart way to ensure that there will be no surprises later on.

GENERAL BUDGET:

Amount from the Wedding Budget set aside for the Honeymoon $ _____

Amount groom is able to contribute from current funds/savings: $ _____

Amount bride is able to contribute from current funds/savings: $ _____

Amount to be saved/acquired by groom from now until the honeymoon date: (monthly contributions, part-time job, gifts, bonuses) $ _____

Amount to be saved/acquired by bride from now until the honeymoon date: (monthly contributions, part-time job, gifts, bonuses) $ _____

GENERAL BUDGET TOTAL AMOUNT: $ _____

CREATING A BUDGET

DETAILED BUDGET

BEFORE THE HONEYMOON

Special clothing purchases: $ _____

Bride's trousseau (honeymoon lin- $ _____
gerie):

Sundries: (HELPFUL HINT: Make $ _____
a list of what you already have and
what you need to purchase. You can
then use these lists as part of your
packing list. See Packing Checklist.)

Film, disposable cameras, extra cam- $ _____
era batteries:

Maps, guide books, travel maga- $ _____
zines:

Foreign language books and tapes, $ _____
translation dictionary:

Passport photos, application fees: $ _____
(See International Travel)

Medical exam, inoculations: (See International Travel) $ _____

Other items: $ _____

Before the Honeymoon Total Amount: $ _____

DURING THE HONEYMOON

Transportation
Airplane tickets: $ _____

Shuttle or cab (to and from the airport): $ _____

Car rental, gasoline, tolls: $ _____

Taxis, buses, other public transportation: $ _____

Transportation Total Amount: $ _____

CREATING A BUDGET

Accommodations

Hotel/resort room (total for entire $ _____
stay):

Room service: $ _____

Miscellaneous "hidden costs": $ _____
Phone use, room taxes and sur-
charges, chambermaid and room
service tips (see Tipping Guide, page
169), in-room liquor bar and snacks.

Accommodations Total Amount: $ **_____**

Meals

Breakfast:
$_____ per meal   x   _____# of days = $_____

Lunch:
$_____ per meal   x   _____# of days = $_____

Casual Dinners:
$_____ per meal   x   _____# of days = $_____

Formal Dinners:

$_____ per meal   x   _____# of days = $_____

Picnics, Snacks:

$_____ per meal   x   _____# of days = $_____

Meals Total Amount: $ _____

Entertainment

Sport and activity lessons: (tennis, $ _____
golf, ballroom dancing, etc.)

Day excursions and tours: (boat $ _____
tours, diving, snorkeling, bus/guided
tours, etc.)

Shows, theater: $ _____

Lounges, nightclubs, discos: (don't $ _____
forget to include the cost of drinks
and bar gratuities)

Museum fees: $ _____

CREATING A BUDGET

Pampering: (massages, spa treat-
ments, hairdresser, etc.) $ _____

Entertainment Total Amount: $ _____

Miscellaneous:

Souvenirs for yourselves: $ _____

Souvenirs and gifts for family and $ _____
friends:

Postcards (including cost of stamps): $ _____

Newspapers and magazines: $ _____

Additional film, replacement sun- $ _____
dries, other:

Miscellaneous Total Amount: $ _____

After the Honeymoon:

Film developing costs: $ _____

Photo albums: $ _____

After the Honeymoon Total Amount: $ _____

For all-inclusives resorts/cruises and travel packages only:

Fill in the entire budget form above
(simply put a $0.00 on the items to
be included in the total package
price), then list the total inclusive
package price on the line above.
Don't forget to include taxes and sur-
charges. $ _____

Inclusive Package Price: $ _____

DETAIL BUDGET TOTAL $ _____
Add all of the subtotals for your
detail budget items.

CREATING A BUDGET

Doing a budget analysis may be one of the most useful things you can do in planning your honeymoon. With all the options available, a good cost analysis will help make the most appropriate decisions very clear to you.

First, create a budget using the previous worksheet for what you think allows for an ideal, yet reasonable, honeymoon. Highlight those expenses which are top priorities. For example, a spacious, ritzy hotel room may be the most important element for you. Or, perhaps participating in numerous sports activities and excursions or enjoying fine dining is more important than a spacious room.

Next, as you come across different destinations and options that appeal to you, fill in a new budget worksheet. Compare the results to other potential trips. See how your priority items on each trip compare to one another. Determine the pros and cons of each. This is also an effective way of looking at the pros and cons of an all-inclusive package versus an independently organized trip.

NOTE: Once you've decided on your honeymoon destination and activities, fill in a new budget as accurately as possible and take it with you on your trip. Use it to chart your expenses as they occur so you will have a visual guide of whether or not you are staying within budget.

If you find that you are going over your budget, take a look at those top priority items that you'd still like to keep. See if you can eliminate some lower priority items to free up some money for the favored ones.

If you find you are under budget, celebrate with a special "gift" for yourselves (massages, an extravagant dinner, another afternoon of jet skiing, etc.)

CREATING A BUDGET

NOTES:

_____

_____

_____

_____

_____

_____

_____

_____

_____

_____

_____

_____

_____

_____

_____

_____

_____

_____

_____

_____

_____

_____

_____

_____

_____

TIPPING GUIDE

This guide is provided to help you get familiar with customary gratuity standards you may encounter throughout your travels.

Tipping customs vary from country to country. It is advisable to inquire about tipping with the international tourism board representing the country you'll be traveling in. Simply ask for information about tipping customs and social expectations. You will also want to discuss gratuities with your travel agent or planner. Some travel packages include gratuities in the total cost, some leave that to the guests, and some even discourage tipping (usually because they have built it into the total package price). Be sure to discuss this with your travel planner.

TIPPING GUIDE

SERVICE	GRATUITY

Air Travel
Skycaps	$1.00 per bag
Flight Attendants	None

Road Travel
Taxi Drivers	15% of fare (no less than 50 cents)
Limousine Driver	15%
Valet Parking	$1.00
Tour Bus Guide	$1.00

Rail Travel
Redcaps	$1.00 per bag (or posted rate plus 50 cents)
Sleeping Car Attendant	$1.00 per person
Train Conductor & Crew	none
Dining Car Attendant	15% of bill

Cruise
Cabin Steward	3 per person per day
Dining Room Waiter	3 per person per day
Busboy	$1.50 per person per day
Maitre d'	At your discretion – recommended $10 - $20
Salon or Spa Personnel	15%
Bartender	$1 - $2 per drink

SERVICE   **GRATUITY**

Restaurants

Maitre d', Head Waiter ....None
      (Unless special services provided, then typically
      $5.00)

Waiter/Waitress ....15% of bill (pretax total)

Bartender ....$1 - $2 per drink

Wine Steward...15% of bill

Washroom Attendant ....$.50 - $1.00

Coat Check Attendant..................................$1.00 per coat
      (NOTE: Some restaurants in foreign countries add
      the gratuity and/or service charge to your bill. If it
      has not been added, tip the customary regional
      rate.)

Hotel/Resort

Concierge ....$2.00 - $10.00
      For special attention or arrangements

Doorman ....$1.00 for hailing taxi

Bellhop................$1.00 per bag + $1.00 for showing room

Room Service ....15% of bill

Chamber Maid...................................$1.00 - $2.00 per day
      or $5.00 - $10.00 per week for longer stays (no tip
      for one-night stays)

SERVICE	GRATUITY

Hotel/Resort (CONT.)

Pool Attendant ....$.50 for towel service

Miscellaneous

Barbershop ....15% of cost

Beauty Salon ....15% of cost

Manicure ....$1.00 - $5.00 depending on cost of service

Facial ....15% of cost

Massage ....15% of cost

THINGS TO PACK

Consider the differences in the climates of where you live now and where you'll be visiting. Also consider the air conditions of airplanes, trains and boats. Bring along items that will help with the transition and keep you feeling as comfortable as possible.

TRAVELERS' FIRST AID KIT

- ❏ Aspirin
- ❏ Antacid tablets
- ❏ Diarrhea medication
- ❏ Cold remedies/sinus decongestant
- ❏ Throat lozenges
- ❏ Antiseptic lotion
- ❏ Band-Aids
- ❏ Moleskin for blisters
- ❏ Breath mints
- ❏ Chapstick

TRAVELERS' FIRST AID KIT (CONT.)

❑ Insect repellent, insect bite medication
❑ Sunblock and sunburn relief lotion
❑ Dry skin lotion/hand cream
❑ Eye drops or eye lubricant
❑ Saline nasal spray, moisturizing nasal spray
❑ Vitamins
❑ Prescription drugs
  NOTE: These should be kept in their original pharmacy containers which provide both drug and doctor information. Be sure to note the drug's generic name. You will want to pack these in your carry on baggage in case the bags you've checked become lost or delayed.
❑ Condoms or other birth control
❑ Physicians' names, addresses and telephone numbers
❑ Health insurance phone numbers
  NOTE: Be sure to contact your provider to find out about coverage while traveling in the U.S. and abroad.
❑ Names and phone numbers of people to contact in case of an emergency.

PACKING CHECKLIST

CARRY ON BAGGAGE

- ☐ Travelers' first aid kit (see previous section)
- ☐ Wallet (credit cards, traveler's checks)
- ☐ Jewelry and other sentimental and valuable items that you feel you must bring
- ☐ Identification (Passport, Driver's License or Photo ID)
- ☐ Photocopies of the following important documents:
  - ☐ Hotel/resort street address, phone number, written confirmation of arrangements and reservations
  - ☐ Complete travel itinerary
  - ☐ Airline tickets
  - ☐ Name, address and phone number of emergency contact person(s) back home
  - ☐ Medicine prescriptions (including generic names) and eyeglass prescription information (or an extra pair); list of food and drug allergies
  - ☐ Phone numbers (including after-hour emergency phone numbers) for health insurance company and personal physicians

PACKING CHECKLIST

CARRY ON BAGGAGE (CONT.)

- ❏ Copy of your packing list. If a piece of your luggage gets lost, you will know the contents that are missing.
- ❏ List of your travelers checks' serial numbers and 24 hour phone number for reporting loss or theft
- ❏ Phone numbers to the local U.S. embassy or consulate
- ❏ Any "essential" toiletries and one complete casual outfit in case checked baggage is delayed or lost
- ❏ Foreign language dictionary or translator
- ❏ Camera with film loaded
- ❏ Maps
- ❏ Small bills/change (in U.S. dollars and in the appropriate foreign currency) for tipping
- ❏ Currency converter chart or pocket calculator
- ❏ Reading material
- ❏ Eyeglasses
- ❏ Contact lenses
- ❏ Contact lens cleaner
- ❏ Sunglasses
- ❏ Kleenex, gum, breath mints and any over-the-counter medicine to ease travel discomfort
- ❏ Inflatable neck pillow (for lengthy travel)
- ❏ Address book and thank you notes (in case you have lots of traveling time)
- ❏ Your Budget Sheet

Other items to carry-on

- ❏ _____
- ❏ _____
- ❏ _____
- ❏ _____
- ❏ _____
- ❏ _____

CHECKED BAGGAGE

CLOTHING

Casual Wear

(Consider the total number of each casual outfit item that you will need)

- ❏ shorts
- ❏ pants
- ❏ tops
- ❏ jackets/sweaters
- ❏ sweatshirts/sweatsuits
- ❏ belts
- ❏ socks
- ❏ underwear/panties & bras
- ❏ walking shoes/sandals/loafers

Casual Wear (CONT.)

❑ _____
❑ _____
❑ _____
❑ _____

Athletic Wear

(Consider the total number of each sporting outfit item that you will need)

❑ shorts
❑ sweatpants
❑ tops
❑ sweatshirts/jackets
❑ swim suits, swim suit cover-up
❑ aerobic activity outfit
❑ athletic equipment
❑ socks
❑ underwear/panties & exercise bras
❑ tennis/athletic shoes
❑ _____
❑ _____
❑ _____
❑ _____

Evening Wear

(Consider the total number of each evening outfit item that you will need)

- ❑ pants or pants/skirts/dresses
- ❑ belts
- ❑ dress shirts/blouses
- ❑ sweaters
- ❑ jackets/blazers/ties
- ❑ socks or pantyhose/slips
- ❑ underwear/panties & bras
- ❑ accessories/jewelry
- ❑ shoes
- ❑ _____
- ❑ _____
- ❑ _____
- ❑ _____

Other Clothing Items

- ❑ pajamas
- ❑ lingerie
- ❑ slippers
- ❑ robe
- ❑ _____
- ❑ _____

PACKING CHECKLIST

MISCELLANEOUS ITEMS

- ❏ An additional set of the important document photo copies as packed in your carry on bag
- ❏ Travel tour books, Tourism Bureau Information
- ❏ Journal
- ❏ Special honeymoon gift for your new spouse
- ❏ Any romantic items or favorite accessories
- ❏ Extra film and camera batteries
- ❏ Plastic bags for dirty laundry
- ❏ Large plastic or nylon tote bag for bringing home new purchases
- ❏ Small sewing kit and safety pins
- ❏ Travel alarm clock
- ❏ Travel iron, Lint brush
- ❏ Compact umbrella, Fold up rain slickers
- ❏ Hand held tape recorder (for recorded memory journal or for bringing along your favorite, romantic tapes) and/or video camera

- ❏ _____
- ❏ _____
- ❏ _____
- ❏ _____

OTHER ITEMS TO BRING

- [ ]
- [ ]
- [ ]
- [ ]
- [ ]
- [ ]
- [ ]
- [ ]
- [ ]
- [ ]
- [ ]
- [ ]
- [ ]
- [ ]
- [ ]
- [ ]
- [ ]
- [ ]
- [ ]
- [ ]

PACKING CHECKLIST

ITEMS TO LEAVE BEHIND
(with a trusted contact person)

- ❑ Photocopy of all travel details (complete itineraries, names, addresses, and telephone numbers)
- ❑ Photocopy of credit cards along with 24-hour telephone number to report loss or theft. (Be sure to get the number to call when traveling abroad. It will be a different number than their U.S. 1 800 number.)
- ❑ Photocopy of travelers checks along with 24-hour telephone number to report loss or theft
- ❑ Photocopy of passport identification page, along with date and place of issuance
- ❑ Photocopy of drivers license
- ❑ Any irreplaceable items

INTERNATIONAL

TRAVEL

There are over 250 U.S. embassies and consulates around the world. After contacting the Tourism Bureau for the area you will be traveling to, it is also a wise idea to contact the U.S. Embassy or Consulate for that region. With assistance from both of these sources you will be able to determine the travel requirements and recommendations for your chosen travel destination. Within this section you will find numerous resources to assure all of your questions and concerns are addressed before you travel. Call for a list of U.S. embassy and consulate locations with emergency phone numbers: (202) 647-5225 or visit http://travel.state.gov

PASSPORTS AND VISAS

Your travel agent should be able to provide you with information to adequately prepare you for your international travels. Additional information (and possibly more detailed and current information) can be obtained by contacting the appropriate sources listed in this section.

As a U.S. citizen, you generally need a passport to enter and to depart most foreign countries and to reenter the United States. Some countries also require Visas. A Visa is an endorsement by officials of a foreign country as permission to visit their country. You first need a passport in order to obtain a Visa. Inquire with the resources listed in this section for requirements of your specific destination.

As mentioned, you will be required to prove your U.S. citizenship upon reentry to the United States. If the country of your destination does not require you to possess a current passport, you will still need to produce proof of citizenship for U.S. Immigration. Items that are acceptable as proof of citizenship include a passport, a certified copy of your Birth certificate, certificate of Nationalization, a Certificate of Citizenship, or a Report of Birth Abroad of a Citizen of the United States. Proof of identification can include a driver's license or a government or military identification card containing a photo or physical description.

NOTE: The bride should have her passport and airline tickets reflect her maiden name for ease in proof of identification while traveling. Name changes can be processed after returning from the honeymoon with your marriage certificate.

Your passport will be one of the most important documents you will take with you. Contact the local U.S. Embassy immediately if your passport becomes lost or stolen. Have a photocopy of your passport's data page, date and place of issuance, and passport number to be kept with a contact person at home. You should also travel with a set of these photocopies in addition to an extra set of loose passport photos for speed in attaining a replacement.

Passports can be obtained from one of the 13 U.S. Passport Agencies (listed later in this section) or one of the thousands of authorized passport locations, such as state and federal courts as well as some U.S. Post Offices (check in the Government Listings section of your phone book).

Currently, the cost to obtain a passport is $65.00 (in person; Form DSP-11) or $55.00 (through the mail; Form DSP-82). If you have had a passport in the past, contact a passport agency to find out if you are eligible to apply through the mail. You will want to apply for your passport several months before your trip, keeping in mind that January through July is a busier time and the process may take longer. In addition to calling the U.S. Passport Agencies for personal assistance, you can also call their 24-hour recorded information lines for information on agency locations, travel advisories and warnings, and Consular Information Sheets pertaining to every country in the world.

Travel Advisory Updates are also available 24-hours a day by calling The Department of State's Office of Overseas Citizens' Services at (202) 647-5225.

Additional, and very helpful, official information for U.S. citizens regarding international travel can be found at http://travel.state.gov

Foreign embassies and consulates located in the U.S. can provide current information regarding their country. You can locate phone numbers and addresses in The Congressional Directory or Foreign Consular Offices in the United States, both available at your local library.

UNITED STATES PASSPORT AGENCIES

http://travel.state.gov/passport_services.html
Inquiries...800-688-9889

Boston Passport Agency
Inquiries.......................................617-565-6990
24-hr info line 617-565-6698

Chicago Passport Agency
Inquiries 312-341-6020
24-hr info line 312-341-6020

Honolulu Passport Agency
Inquiries.......................................808-522-8283
24-hr info line 808-522-8283

Houston Passport Agency
Inquiries.......................................713-751-0294
24-hr info line 713-751-0294

Los Angeles Passport Agency
Inquiries...... 310-235-7075
24-hr info line 310-235-7070

UNITED STATES PASSPORT AGENCIES (CONT.)

Miami Passport Agency

Inquiries..305-859-2705

24-hr info line 305-859-2705

New Orleans Passport Agency

Inquiries..504-412-2600

24-hr info line ....,,,,,,   504 512 2600

New York Passport Agency

Inquiries..212-374-0615

24-hr info line 212-374-0615

Philadelphia Passport Agency

Inquiries..215-597-7480

24-hr info line 215-597-7480

San Francisco Passport Agency

Inquiries..415-744-5627

24-hr info line 415-538-2700

Seattle Passport Agency

Inquiries..206-808-5700

24-hr info line 206-808-5700

UNITED STATES PASSPORT AGENCIES (CONT.)

Stamford Passport Agency

  Inquiries..203-969-9000

  24-hr info line 206-969-9000

Washington Passport Agency

  Inquiries..202-647-0518

  24-hr info line 202-647-0518

Some private sources offering assistance in obtaining a passport (usually offering expedited service):

International Visa Service.............................800-627-1112

World Wide Visas 800-527-1861

Travel Document Systems 800-874-5100

or www.traveldocs.com

HEALTH CONCERNS

In the United States the National Center for Infectious Diseases (NCID) and the Centers for Disease Control (CDC) provide the most current information pertinent to international travel. The World Health Organization (WHO) concerns itself with general and specific health issues for almost every part of the world. Health and safety issues as related to international travel are the basis for the International Heath Regulations adopted by the World Health Organization.

Your travel agent should be fully informed about current conditions and requirements. Your personal physician should also be able to provide you with health-related information and advice for traveling in the region you visit. You can personally obtain very useful (and very thorough) information from the Center for Disease Control and Prevention (CDC). The CDC's Travelers' Health Section has the following useful resources:

Health Information for International Travel
("The Yellow Book") Available from:
The Superintendent of Documents
U.S. Government Printing Office

Washington, D.C. 20402

202-512-1800 or download a free copy at
www.cdc.gov

**Summary of Health Information for International
Travel** ("The Blue Sheet")A biweekly publication
available by fax: 404-332-4565 (request document
220022#)

For updates and changes by phone or fax, call (404) 332-
4559 or visit www.cdc.gov.

TRAVELERS' HEALTH INSURANCE COVERAGE

If your health insurance policy does not cover you abroad,
consider acquiring a temporary health insurance policy.
Travel agencies, health insurance companies, travelers'
check companies and your local phone book should be able
to provide names of relevant companies for you. In addition
to health insurance coverage, many policy packages also
include protection in case of trip cancellation and baggage
loss.

Keep prescription medications in their original pharmacy

containers with the original labels. Bring a copy of your prescriptions and note the drug's generic name. You may consider getting a letter from your physician warranting your need for the medication.

CUSTOMS

The following list contains some useful publications regarding customs and custom policies when traveling internationally:

> **Know Before You Go; Customs Hints for Returning U.S. Residents**
> U.S. Customs
> P.O. Box 7407
> Washington, D.C. 20004
> 202-566-8195

> **Travelers' Tips on Bringing Food, Plant and Animal Products into the United States**
> U.S. Department of Agriculture
> 613 Federal Building
> 6505 Belcrest Road
> Hyattsville, MD 20782

An Unwanted Souvenir; Lead in Ceramic Ware

U.S. Food and Drug Administration
HFI-40
Rockville, MD 20857

NOTES:

THINGS TO DO FOR

YOUR HONEYMOON

DONE	TO DO
❏	
❏	
❏	
❏	
❏	
❏	
❏	
❏	
❏	
❏	
❏	
❏	
❏	
❏	
❏	

THINGS TO DO - HONEYMOON

DONE	TO DO
❏	
❏	
❏	
❏	
❏	
❏	
❏	
❏	
❏	
❏	
❏	
❏	
❏	
❏	
❏	
❏	
❏	
❏	
❏	
❏	
❏	

THINGS TO DO - HONEYMOON

DONE   **TO DO**

❏ _____

❏ _____

❏ _____

❏ _____

❏ _____

❏ _____

❏ _____

❏ _____

❏ _____

❏ _____

❏ _____

❏ _____

❏ _____

❏ _____

❏ _____

❏ _____

❏ _____

❏ _____

❏ _____

❏ _____

❏ _____

THINGS TO DO - HONEYMOON

DONE　　　　**TO DO**

❏

❏

❏

❏

❏

❏

❏

❏

❏

❏

❏

❏

❏

❏

❏

❏

❏

❏

❏

❏

THINGS TO DO - HONEYMOON

DONE   **TO DO**

☐ _____

☐ _____

☐ _____

☐ _____

☐ _____

☐ _____

☐ _____

☐ _____

☐ _____

☐ _____

☐ _____

☐ _____

☐ _____

☐ _____

☐ _____

☐ _____

☐ _____

☐ _____

☐ _____

☐ _____

☐ _____

THINGS TO DO - HONEYMOON

DONE	TO DO
❏	
❏	
❏	
❏	
❏	
❏	
❏	
❏	
❏	
❏	
❏	
❏	
❏	
❏	
❏	
❏	
❏	
❏	
❏	
❏	
❏	

WEDDING SOLUTIONS

The largest and most respected wedding
publishing and consulting company in America
Proudly Presents

 # WEDDINGSOLUTIONS.COM

FOR ALL YOUR WEDDING NEEDS

Voted the most comprehensive and easy-
to-use website by brides nationwide!

What is WeddingSolutions.com?

WeddingSolutions.com is the most comprehensive and easy-
to-use website for brides planning their wedding. We cover
every aspect of wedding planning, from start to finish. Find
everything you need in one convenient location.

Why use WeddingSolutions.com?

Because *WeddingSolutions.com* has features not offered by
any other wedding website on the market. From the
moment of engagement to your honeymoon, we offer
resources, helpful hints, and wedding planning tools to make
wedding planning as easy as it can be.

Log onto *www.WeddingSolutions.com* for details.

WeddingSolutions.com

FOR ALL YOUR WEDDING NEEDS

For over 13 years, Wedding Solutions has been helping brides and grooms across the nation plan the most memorable day of their life. With over 1.5 million Wedding Solutions books in print, we have become America's leader in the wedding planning industry.

WeddingSolutions.com offers features not found in other wedding sites, including personalized wedding consulting, honeymoon registry, and request for quotes and special offers from thousands of local vendors, reception and honeymoon sites.

Planning your wedding can be an overwhelming, stressful, and time consuming process. That is why we created *WeddingSolutions.com*. It will save you time, money, and a lot of stress. Visit us and see how easy wedding planning can be!

Log onto *www.WeddingSolutions.com* for details.

WEDDINGSOLUTIONS.COM

FOR ALL YOUR WEDDING NEEDS

*E*verything you need
to plan the wedding of your dreams!

- ❦ Wedding Planning Tools
- ❦ Largest Online Wedding Store
- ❦ Thousands of Resources:
    - •Local Vendors
    - •Reception Sites
    - •Honeymoon Destinations
- ❦ Gift Registry
- ❦ Honeymoon Registry
- ❦ Book Your Travel
- ❦ Create Your Own Website
- ❦ Chat Room
- ❦ Bulletin Board
- ❦ Free Newsletters
- ❦ Fashion and Beauty Tips
- ❦ Free Online Photo Album
- ❦ And Much More

*C*ome and see how
easy wedding planning can be!

WeddingSolutions.com

FOR ALL YOUR WEDDING NEEDS

Personalized Wedding Consultant

Elizabeth Lluch, author of 19 bestselling wedding planning books,
will guide you through every step of your wedding planning:

- Budget Analysis
- Stationery Items
- Print Envelopes
- Checklists
- Guest List
- Timelines
- Service Providers
- Seating Arrangements
- Gifts Received & More

The Largest Online Wedding Store

The largest selection of over 2,000 of the most beautiful and
unique wedding products, accessories, gifts, and more:

- Invitations
- Cameras
- Cake Tops
- Jewelry
- Favors
- Bubbles
- Unity Candles
- Toasting Glasses
- Cake Knives
- Ring Pillows
- Engravable Items
- & More

Find Local Vendors

See and compare prices, experience, policies, references, and
photographs. Request quotes and special offers from thousands of:

- Videographers
- Florists
- Caterers
- Photographers
- Bakers
- Musicians
- Wedding Consultants
- Transportation
- & More

Find Reception & Honeymoon Sites

Request quotes, compare prices, receive special offers, and view
information on thousands of reception & honeymoon sites worldwide.

- Reception Packages
- View Facilities
- Surrounding Areas
- Honeymoon Packages
- Request Information
- Policies
- Amenities
- Packages
- & More

Log onto *www.WeddingSolutions.com* for details.

WEDDINGSOLUTIONS.COM

FOR ALL YOUR WEDDING NEEDS

Bride's Community

Our wedding community is a place where brides across the U.S. can come together to lend support to each other.

- Chat Room
- Newsletters
- Featured Articles
- Advice Column
- Bulletin Board
- Fashion & Beauty

Register for Your Honeymoon

Register for monetary gifts toward your honeymoon. Your guests will appreciate this convenient way to contribute towards your:

- Airfare
- Meals
- Tours
- Hotel Accommodations
- Recreation & Activities
- Entertainment
- Rentals
- Spa Treatments
- & More

Wedding Website

Easily create your very own wedding website. Share with your guests what you are planning for your wedding and beyond!

- How you met
- Advice for guests
- Post a photo
- How you got engaged
- Wedding Details
- Links to related sites
- Your future plans
- Online Guest Book
- & Much more

Book Your Travel

Take care of all your travel arrangements, from locating the perfect destination, to booking tickets, hotels, and more. We offer the lowest prices on the following:

- Cruises
- Resorts
- All inclusives
- Private villas
- Unique Places
- Golf Packages
- Car Rentals
- Special Offers

Log onto *www.WeddingSolutions.com* for details.

Voted the most comprehensive and

WEDDINGSOLUTIONS.COM

FOR ALL YOUR WEDDING NEEDS

What is Wedding Solutions Publishing?

Wedding Solutions is the largest and most respected wedding planning and publishing company in America. We have been in business for over ten years and have helped millions of brides and grooms plan the wedding of their dreams through our best selling wedding planning books.

Easy Wedding Planner Organizer & Keepsake............................U.S. $29.95

Easy Wedding Planning ....U.S. $9.95

Easy Wedding Planning Plus ....U.S. $19.95

The Ultimate Groom's Guide...U.S. $9.95

The

The **395.22 Llu**

The **Lluch, Elizabeth.**

The **The ultimate groom's guide**

The

The

The

The Ultimate Wedding Planning Guide ....U.S. $19.95

The Very Best Wedding Planner & Organizer ...............................U.S. $26.95

The Very Best Wedding Planning Guide ....U.S. $26.95

Wedding Party Responsibility Cards ....U.S. $9.95

Wedding Solutions Books are sold at all major bookstores, such as Barnes & Noble, Borders, Waldenbooks, B Dalton and Books-A-Million. You can also see complete details on these books when you log onto *www.WeddingSolutions.com*.

Log onto *www.WeddingSolutions.com* for details.